1

Irish Blood and Grit
By Peter McDonagh

This book is dedicated to my sister Tish and my brother Liam and my boxing teacher Steve Hiser
-Peter McDonagh

Chapter 1
Where it all began

On a cold December night, four sleeps before Christmas, a fighter was born at the Galway General Hospital. To be exact, it was four minutes past four in the afternoon on December 21, 1977, when I, Peter McDonagh drew my first breath. My mother and father were both born in Cararoe, a Gaelic Irish speaking village in Connemara on the west coast of Ireland.

The first memory of my then 43-year-old father (Bill), was that he was around 6 ft, slim, with jet black hair, and had massive shovel like hands. Dad was a very softly spoken man, and pretty laid back. My mum, in contrast, was aged 33 and around 5 ft 3 with short brown hair. The thing I remember most about mum was that she was very confident, and definitely the boss of the house. I also recall that she was around five months pregnant at the time. We lived in what seemed like a massive four bedroom bungalow with a huge front room, kitchen and a lovely open turf fire.

Our house sat on the top of a hill overlooking 16 acres of land, where we raised our own Connemara ponies, cows, chickens, goats and sheep. Somebody had to keep all those animals in check and that was the job of our sheepdog, Blackie.

It really was a beautiful picture-postcard type place, and being surrounded by the sea made it all the more special. We lived off our land, producing eggs, milk, meat and fish. What we could not produce ourselves we bought from the mobile shopper, who called around once a week to deliver bread, coco and flour.

I will never forget, we used to wait on the hill for the van to pull up. When I look back it was paradise living in such a beautiful but simple place. It was a place where people used to travel to the bank on the back of a horse and cart. I remember us all sitting in the front room in the evening, with the rain, wind and thunder and lightning belting off the windows, like waves hitting the rocks. No matter how bad the weather was on the west coast of Ireland we always felt safe and warm in front of a big open fire with my mum and dad sitting in their armchairs and, Tish and Liam sitting on the sofa drinking cocoa and making each other laugh. Tish was 11years old, small, with mousey long blond hair, blue eyes and a cheeky big smile, that was always lovingly directed towards me and Liam.

Liam was aged 10, had light brown hair, freckles and big blue eyes, and was a very quiet lad. Then there was me, five years old, tiny, with strawberry blonde hair and a face full of freckles. Just like Tish and Liam, I too had that cheeky McDonagh smile but I also had a voice you could hear from the house, all the way to the seafront. I was always playing tricks as well, just like the little Leprechaun I was brought up to be.

Both Tish and Liam spoke English and Gaelic because they were born in London, England. My mum and Dad lived there for a few years but my dad had to return home with the family to care for his sick mum at the family home. Then I came along and not long after, my grandmother died following a long illness. The land and house were left to my dad. He had brothers and sisters, but they were all doing well in life and my dad's oldest brother. Poric was the beneficiary of the Will. By tradition the eldest family member always inherited the estate. That's how things were done in Ireland in those days. Poric called a meeting with the family and said, "it's only right that Bill had the land signed over to him. Not only did he look after our mum, but he left his home in England with his wife and children to take care of mum, so I'm signing the house and land over to him".

I used to love going to work with my dad. He could not get a job as work was few and far between in Connemara back in the 1970s. That's why he moved to the UK in the first place. So, he made use of the sea and used to pick periwinkles. Not an easy job but it was a little bit of money to keep us going. We lived a stone's throw from the beach, just a short walk across the rocky land and onto the Dolin beach. I would run across the sand and onto my favourite rock while my dad went into the shallow water with his bag to collect periwinkles. I would play on the rocks, rain, wind or shine. I never wore shoes or a shirt a lot of the time, just shorts.

Living by the sea was magical but we were always warned about the dangers of the sea. By that I mean the tides, and the fast flowing waves. I would sit there for six to eight hours a day watching the roaring waves smash off the rocks. One day my dad must have forgotten I was with him as he would sometimes leave the house very early. But I would get up as well and even run out the door in just my underpants. I would call Blackie, run across the land, onto the beach and make for my favourite rock. Dad used to work with the tides and call me back before my rock got surrounded by the incoming tide. But this particular day was very different. It was a stormy day as usual, and I was sitting on my rock watching the sea and throwing stones while watching dad. Suddenly I looked up and the rain had stopped. In its place was a beautiful rainbow, so I called my dad and he looked up. I was pointing to the sky, and he screamed. I then noticed my Rock was surrounded by water. My dad was panicking and ran to get help. I could swim but I was only five, and from rock to shore was around 50 metres. It may as well have been 500 metres away for a little fella like me. Whilst I looked back up at the rainbow, flashing through my mind was how dangerous the sea could be. I took a deep breath; jumped in and swam for my life. It felt like I was never going to get to the safety of the shore. When my dad returned from finding help, I was lying on the beach and breathing very heavily. Dad asked me if I was okay and then gave me one hell of a talking to. "I told you how dangerous that water is". I looked up and said with my best cheeky McDonagh smile "I told you I'm a good swimmer." Once we had arrived home, I had never been so please than to see Blackie sitting there wagging his tail.

One day me and Liam were playing outside while Tish was inside cleaning. I had a calf called Ginger. Liam tied a bit of rope around Ginger's neck and put me in a big plastic fishing box. Liam tied the rope to the handle of the box and smacked the calf on the bum, hard with

9

another piece of rope and Ginger ran off like a thoroughbred racehorse. There I was flying along enjoying myself when the fishing box flipped over, sending me flying through the air. Liam got scared and went running towards the glass patio doors where Tish was still cleaning. it was a sunny day and there was a reflection of the sun on the glass but Tish had done such a great job cleaning the window, that Liam thought the closed patio door was open and run straight through it.

As I come up the hill crying from my injury Tish was screaming. Liam looked like she had tipped a bucket of ketchup over his head, he was cut that badly. The hospital was an hour away so mum got him in the car, whilst at the same time screaming, "you're a silly boy, could you not see the glass? I stayed at home with Tish. When Liam came back, he looked like a mummy. He was bandaged all around his head. The Doctor said he was lucky he only had 30 stitches because if the glass had penetrated his neck, it could have killed him. It was scary and it took a while but a few months later we all saw the funny side.

One night we were all sitting around the fire. I was showing Tish and Liam my new school shoes mum had bought. Tish said, "does anyone want some cocoa? As she went to the kitchen; Liam went to the toilet. To this day I do not know why but I decided to throw one of my school shoes into the fire and put the other one back into the box.

On the morning of my first day at school, Tish was dressing me, and Mum said, "where are your shoes, Pete?' I said, "I don't know." Tish said, "They are in the box." My mum picked up the box, opened it and said, "where is the other one?' I shrugged my shoulders; she started screaming at me and I just burst out crying. I pointed to the fire and said, "It's in there (pointing to the fire)". "Why have you done that", Mum shouted back. I replied, "I don't want to go to school. I want to go to work with dad".
So, mum sent me to school with one shoe on, and I cried all the way there. That day did not quite work out how I would have liked!

One night mum came home after a night out with friends (she was heavily pregnant at this point) and my dad had just finished work. We could hear her shouting from the bedroom and heard my dad saying: "we can't do this to the kids". Almost immediately my dad came into the room and said, "pack as many bags as you can carry." My mum rushed in behind him and Tish asked: "where are we going? Mum answered very aggressively, "Don't worry about where we're fucking going, just pack your fucking bags." Tish took our hands, led us into the bedroom, and helped us pack our bags. Then we all got into the car with tears running down our cheeks. We were then told that we were moving back to London.

Chapter 2
From Paradise to poverty

When we arrived in London, we moved in with our cousins. There was nine of us in a two-bedroom flat, so you can imagine how much of a squeeze that was. At first, it felt like we were on holiday. It was only for a few weeks whilst we were waiting for alternative accommodation A short while later, we moved into emergency accommodation at Giles House on the Dickens estate, just off the Old Jamaica Road, in the heart of Bermondsey, south London. We got out of the car; I looked up at the block facing us and then looked over each shoulder. There were two blocks identical to our flats and in the middle was a park, if you want to call it that. All there was, were a few swings, a roundabout, and a concrete ship, and not a bit of grass in sight. No sooner had I got over the sight of the so-called playground area, we were greeted by someone shouting out of a window: 'Fuck off to where you came from you fucking Paddy's'. We had only been in Bermondsey for five minutes and already we were being told to fuck off back to where we came from. I think the battered car with Irish plates must have given us away!

What window or balcony the racist abuse came from was anyone's guess but the voice echoed around the estate, 'you're not welcome here!' Then on the third floor, facing us, a friendly Irish voice shouted over, 'Take no notice of those black and tans, your living next door to us.' I took a deep breath and pictured in my mind how we had come from such a beautiful part of the Irish coast to what on first impressions, seemed like a battleground where only the fittest survived. Thinking about it now, it was 1983 and the IRA at that point were blowing London to pieces. So, it was no surprise we were getting racist comments. Our Irish neighbours shouted over the balcony, 'come up and have a cup of tea? So, we got in the lift and made our way. An overwhelming disgusting smell hit me immediately as I entered and I said to Tish, 'Have you done a wee?' My dad looked down at me and said, 'It's the lift. 'What do you mean,' I replied. Dad said people have been using the lift as a toilet. That was the last day I got in that lift. The stairs didn't smell much better, either but at least I kept on the move. We went to the neighbours; the mum and dad were called Joe and Maisie and looked the same age or similar to dad and mum. They had four kids, Jason,15, Martin 14, Marcella 13, and Seanad, 11. They had a nice three-bedroom flat. The four kids showed us around. Joe said: 'your flat's the same'. There was a back balcony joined to ours, not very big. I asked if I could go out there. Martin said: 'Dad ill show Pete, Liam and Tish around. So out we went. For me, it was a great road. Below us we could see fast, flash cars going past and people walking into shops. Opposite was some railway arches; trains were running more or less 24 hours a day in and out of London Bridge station. Three floors up I felt I could touch the sky, I felt like the king of the castle for a brief moment, but I soon came crashing down again after smelling all those fumes.

Being in Bermondsey and breathing in all that pollution was in complete contrast to being back home in Connemara and walking out the front door onto the hill to taste the salt of the sea and taking in the beautiful coastal views with all the animals.

We came back in off the balcony, and I looked at my dad and said: 'I love Bermondsey'. Joe asked, "Do you want a drink?" I said, "Yes please," thinking it would be either tea, coffee or a cold drink. But to my surprise, out comes a bottle of coke. it tasted amazing, I never drunk fizzy drinks before, so I experienced a serious sugar rush. Bermondsey was getting better by the minute. Joe asked, "When is your furniture being delivered?" My mum said, "My brother is bringing it this evening". At that moment, a giant lorry appeared downstairs. My dad ran down with Liam and Tish before my neighbour (Joe) could put his shoes on. Tish and Liam had the suitcases out of the back of the lorry and my dad pulled out a single mattress. He shut the door on the back of the lorry and it left as quickly as it had arrived. Joe shouted over the balcony, "Is that everything

13

Bill?" Bill shouted back, "Yes." Joe looked at his wife Maisie and said, "These poor people have got nothing". More shouting off another balcony, someone said sarcastically,
"Size of that lorry and Fuck all in it. They will fuck off in a few weeks them tinkers".

Dad, Tish, Liam and my mum returned upstairs and opened the door to our new flat When dad came in with our bags and single mattress it was just a shell and felt cold. I asked if we had got any turf for the fire as it was freezing in there. Dad said: "Pete no fire here". Joe and Maisie came in from next door with some gifts of cups, plates, cutlery and some warm thick tiger blankets. Tish put one around me and whispered in my ear, "Things will get better".

First night in our flat, me, Liam and Tish huddled up in the tiger blanket on the single mattress. mum slept next door at joe and Maisie's as she was weeks away from having the baby. Dad slept on the floor next to us. None of us slept a wink as we were not used to the trains from London Bridge coming past our window, and cars and lorry's roaring past all night, as well as the bright streetlights, lighting up the night sky. And were people screaming all night, it was so different from the pure darkness and silence we were used to back home in Connemara. After waking up on the first morning in our new flat, Joe came in and suggested he and my dad go down to the Salvation Army to get some furniture. Joe then took us to meet our other neighbours on the other side of us. Her name was Elaine and she had two kids, Tina and Paul. At the end of the balcony was a family called the Chilian's. They were from Mexico. They were really crazy, but very nice people.

The neighbours directly underneath us were from Kingston, Jamaica. Shirley, the mum was around my mum's age. She had hair like Don King (the American boxing promoter). She had a daughter, Sharon, who was around the same age as Tish. They became friends. Shirley said to my dad, "Irish and blacks stick together around here, if you ever need anything, give me a knock. I've been here a few years and got connections in Peckham and Brixton".

My mum and dad said thank you and dad and Joe went off to the Salvation Army. A few moments later there was a knock at the door, it

14

was Marcella and Seanad. They brought some bits and pieces from their flat that they thought we may need. They went back and forth for ages bringing us stuff. Within a few hours, they must have given us half the contents they owned. I think they just felt sorry for us and wanted to make us feel at home as my mum was about to have a baby at any time.

Not long after Jason and Martin arrived. They were keen to show us the shops at the bottom of the block. Me, Tish and Liam were only too happy to explore so off we went.

No sooner had we got to the bottom of the communal stairs and onto the roadside, I noticed it was like nothing we had ever experienced before. There was a second-hand shop, Hairdressers, a Launderette and my particular favourite, a sweet shop.

As you can imagine, there were not many shops in our sleepy village back home, let alone a row of them. By the end of the week, I was on first name terms with the sweet shop owners. A lady called Barbara ran the shop with her son, Bryan. It was like something out of Willy Wonka's Chocolate Factory. I loved it there.

I particularly liked the 10p Pick n Mix and always remember Bryan joking with me that he had to go down to the cellar and get some more stock. It took me six months to realise that there was no cellar. Brian was just winding me up by walking and bending his knees at the same time. It looked bloody real to a gullible little fella like me!

After we got back from the shops that first day, Dad and Joe soon followed with a van full to the brim with beds, chairs, rugs, an oven and a brown sofa bed. I, Liam and Tish slept on the sofa bed. It took a few weeks to get the curtains sorted so had to make do with black dustbin bags for the time being to block out the light. It felt just like being back in Connemara. The one thing we could not erase, though was the noise from outside. It got even worse a short time later with the arrival of my new sibling, Martin McDonagh. He had lungs Like the opera singer, Pavarotti.

Chapter 3
Bullied at school.

Little Martin's arrival co-in sided with me starting at my new school. The night before, Jason and Martin came round to the flat and sat me down. "Pete", they said, "Tomorrow you become a big boy. You're on your own but remember, be proud of where you come from and never let people bully you. Hold your head high and chest out".

I looked at them and smiled but if I'm honest, inside I was scared. I was six years old on my first day at St Joseph's Primary School. Liam and Tish were in the big school down the road at St Michael's. They were fine because not only did they have each other but Martin, Jason, Sinead and Marcella were there as well, but I was on my own. And to make things worse it was freezing cold and I was wearing my short trousers.

I was from Connemara where it rains at least 250 days of the year so as far as I was concerned the London streets of Bermondsey were sunny all year round.

I will never forget my first day at school. I could see and hear the other kids taking the piss out of me. Things like, 'Look at that stupid Irish boy in shorts, can't your mum get you proper shoes? Mum and dad did their best but we could only afford clothes from the second-hand shop and my shoes were three sizes too big. I was picked up by my mum, who met me with my new little brother, Martin. I had tears in my eyes, mum said, "what's wrong? I said, "I want to go home". She replied, "you are home". I quickly fired back in an angry tone, "No, Connemara is home". "Don't be silly, this is your home now," mum shouted back.

I cried all the way home and mum never said a word. I could not wait to walk through the front door and take off those over sized Monkey boots. Being at school that first day was the first time I witnessed that sort of mental abuse, and it was not going to be my last.

I waited at the window that first day for Tish and Liam to come home with tears rolling down my cheeks. As they both came through the front door smiling, Tish saw me bawling my eyes out and worryingly said, "what's the matter? I said, "nothing" but she knew and gave me a cuddle. I told her I hated it here and wanted to go home. Tish was always my comforting influence and softly whispered in my ear, "It will be ok, stay strong". No sooner had Tish offered those encouraging words, Jason came in from next door with a big smile on his face. "How was school". Liam and Tish said it was 'ok'. Jason looked at me, but I never replied. "Ah, not so good for Pete then". I told him they keep calling me names and Jason said, "remember what me and Martin said". I looked at them just and smiled. The mental abuse went on for a few weeks at school but then it went up a level when the physical attacks started, and I was getting beaten up on regular basis. I was coming home with bruises, bite marks, black eyes, pretty much whole set. As soon as my mum found out what was going on, she went up to the school and spoke to the head teacher.

The physical attacks and mental abuse stopped for a few months but by this time there was a turning point at home and mum started to hit the bottle quite hard while dad was out working every hour God sent to make a better life and put food on the table. Tish was kept home from school to look after Martin. Then the abuse started up at school again. That was bad enough but when I came home mum was pretty much always pissed, screaming, hitting my dad and smashing things up. It became pretty common place for me, Liam and Tish to be huddled up in the corner, frightened at what was going on. Then mum would go out all night, leaving my dad waiting up until she came home, before he went off to work.

By now, Tish was becoming more and more like a mother to me. She was only 14, herself but she was the one dressing me in the morning and taking me to school with my little brother, Martin in his pram. I cannot ever remember getting a cuddle from my mum, it was always Tish.

In school, I did try and stick up for myself but it was always five onto one. Every time I got knocked down, I kept getting up and thinking, 'Is that all you got'. I really did just want to cry and say, 'just leave me alone', I come to school to get away from the abuse at home'. But just like Martin and Jason told me, I always walked away with my head held high and my chest out.

Any Irish person will tell you that your Holy Communion is one of the most important occasions in a family's history. But when mine came around I was dreading it because by this time my mum was getting drunk on a daily basis. But she promised Dad that she would not be getting pissed up on my big day. Those were famous last words because the night before she was pissed as a fart once again. I cannot say I was surprised!

I pleaded for Tish to take me to my Communion, but mum insisted she was going to because she was my mum and that I should be proud of her. That morning Dad came into the bedroom room at about 5am, kissed me on the head, and said, "enjoy today, Daddy's got to go to work". I never slept a wink thinking about the day ahead and what was in store for me.

Again, Tish took me to school with Martin in the pram as mum was still in bed, pissed from the night before. I was very quiet all the way. The odd tear but Tish cuddled me as we went to church for my holy communion. I was looking around for mum, but she was nowhere to be seen. When I got back to school after my holy communion, I was just about to have my photo taken on the grass verge at the back of the school when my mum stumbled in the worse for wear. Everyone was looking around laughing. Thinking back now it was just like something out of a comedy sketch from the TV. As the cameraman said 'Smile', I'm looking at my mum and I can't believe it. The cameraman turns around and she walks up to me with her high heels sticking in the grass and make up all over the shop. As she got to me, she grabs hold of me by the hand. I looked her straight in the eyes and shouted, "you promised you would not be drunk".

She gave me one of her sterns looks, before digging her nails in my hand and said, "just smile". Mum's nails dug in so viciously, my hand bled. I wanted to scream. I still have that picture today and you can see the pain in my eyes. I still carry the physical as well as the mental scares to this day. I was just eight years old and thought it was normal, having watched her smack Tish and Liam and pull their hair. I thought it was just another normal day in the McDonagh house.

Quite often when we were out of the house we would go to the local park with Seanad and Marcella and play on the swings.

One particular Sunday afternoon Dad was looking after my little brother, Martin so Tish could join us in the park. Mum was in the pub as usual and we were having a great time. As we were playing, we heard a lot of screaming from the block opposite. Tish said, "It sounds like mum". Then we heard a voice shouting, 'fuck off back to Ireland you piss head. Wait till my son gets home we will come up to your flat and kick your husband's fucking head in'.

Quick as a flash we ran upstairs to warn dad. He told us to go to our room and lock the door. We did as he asked and all cuddled up in the corner. My dad is a very placid man, just a hard-working polite man that works on the roads. Moments later the front door crashes open and my piss head of a mum stumbles in, totally incoherent. After some choice words, a bit of cupboard slamming and a few broken cups later, dad managed to get her to bed but not before sustaining a few scratches and slaps along the way.

After a while, we were brave enough to peep out of a crack in the bedroom door. The whole place fell silent. Mum had passed out on the bed so we went to the living room and sat with Dad. He would never say a bad word about Mum. "She's just had a bit too much to drink," he would say. Dad was just trying his best to keep things as normal as possible for us kids.

A couple of hours later there is an almighty knock on the door. As we looked out of the window, we see the man from across the block with his two sons. I started screaming but Tish put her hand over my mouth and told me to be quiet. The banging stopped and there is silence apart from faint voices outside. 'Let's kick the door in and do the Irish bastards,' I heard one of them say.

Dad quickly turned to Tish and said, "Take Martin in your room and don't come out". Martin was about 15 months old then I think. I had a Hurley, it's like a hockey stick and was my pride and joy. dad picked it up. I had never seen him as angry as he was that day. Dad was a gentleman but his back was against the wall. By now the door seemed like it was going to be kicked in so dad ran to the door followed by us screaming kids. As he opens the door, dad raised the Hurley above his head and just snapped. "I've just about had enough," as he marched forward to take out the dad and his two kids. One of the three shouted, "He's fucking mental", as he stood back from the swinging Hurley.

Dad said, "you got two choices; you can turn around and go down the stairs and never come near my door again or I will chuck you over the balcony". They chose to turn around and ran down the stairs. That was the last time trouble came to our door. As soon as they left, the door went again. And again, my heart nearly jumped out of my mouth. We were lucky this time, though, it was Shirley from downstairs.

"What's happened, Bill? I could hear all the noise". Dad told her what had happened and she whispered in his ear that she could get him a gun if he needs one. Shirley did not think I could hear her but I did. My dad replied, firmly, "No, don't be silly they won't come back".

Shirley said, "if they do, I'll get you one and they won't come back again". Dad just smiled. As the word spread around that the Irish family 'is mad', Dad got a bit more respect.

Chapter 4
From bad to worse

Although we were left alone on the estate after dad's made moment, nothing changed for me at school. I was still being bullied and being called a Leprechaun. I did not mind that but words like thick Paddy was not nice. I took a real bad beating one day. I was around eight and a half. I was on lunch break and two kids come at me from behind, got me around the neck and pulled me to the floor. Another group came over and started kicking me all over my body.

I was covering my face but a stray boot found its way straight up my bollocks. I never felt pain like it I can tell you. I honestly thought I was going to die. As I put my hands down to protect my crown jewels, I caught a Monkey boot straight between the eyes. The bruises came up pretty quickly and it was not long before I resembled one of those Pandas at London Zoo.

When I got back in the classroom the teacher quickly pulled me to one side to ask what had happened? I suspect she already knew I'd taken a kicking but I said I had run into a goal post while I was playing football.

The teacher took me straight down to the Nurse's room to check me over. I suppose it must have looked pretty serious to them because the Nurse rang for an ambulance and I was rushed off to Guys Hospital. As usual Mum was in no fit state to come and get me so Tish hopped onto a bus to pick me up. I told Tish the same story I told the teachers.

At this point, we were starting to settle in a bit and joined a club called Fisher Downside Youth. Liam joined partly to socialise with new people but mainly to escape from the violence at home. Poor Tish never had a choice. No way was Mum letting her go to the club with Liam because

21

she was 'Mum' to me and Martin. I asked Liam one day if he would take me. So, we asked Mum, and she said Yes, so off we went.

I liked those few hours of an evening at the club because I could just forget about the abuse and volatile atmosphere at home, and the bullying and physical attacks at school. We used to go swimming, play snooker and football as well. And do you know what? I never walked into a goal post once, lol.

Things were starting to look up a bit after a while. Not only was I enjoying being part of a group at the youth club, but we also moved away from Giles House as well, to a four-bedroom ground floor Maisonette. Tish and Liam loved it there as they only had to roll out of bed, and they were at the school gates. The school was only on the other side of Jamaica Road. It was sad to leave our neighbours and the block but moving into Wrayburn House was a lot more inviting. Even school was getting more bearable as well. I was becoming a cockney. A Bermondsey Boy that had language all of its own.

At home, nothing changed. When dad was working, mum was still getting pissed. She would hit us, kids, quite a bit but it was Tish that was targeted the most, mainly because she was trying to protect us. Mum was pretty brutal to Tish, pulling her hair out and even attacked her with an Iron, once as well.

We made a few friends straight away in the block where we lived. Even School was going well, and we were still going up the Fisher. But not everyone in the McDonagh household was settling in as well. Tish always said things would get better for us and I was starting to think she was right but, unfortunately Mum continued to make her life a misery.

Things came to a head when my Mum's Brother was getting married in Bermondsey. As Tish was getting me and Martin ready, we could hear shouting and swearing from mum and dad's room. Something was going on which I guess was just the start of what was to come. Once we were dressed, Tish got herself ready. By now we were all waiting downstairs for Tish to come down. When she did Mum was angry and said, "What do you think you have got on, get back upstairs and get changed".

This was the first time I had noticed that Mum was actually jealous of her own daughter. I think that's one of the reasons why she beat her and would not let her out with her friends.

Off we went to the wedding. We were having a great time dancing and running about like kids do on these occasions when about three hours later a fight broke out and I saw my dad in the middle of it.

There was An Irish family there called the Dulgans. The mum Bridie, obviously saw what was going on and took my hand to lead me away. I said "where's Tish, Liam and Martin? she said they had already left. They had a son called John, who was the same age as me. Bridie insisted I go and stay with them for the night, so after a little bribe involving some Chocolate, I agreed. Off I went with a smile on my face.

I remember John had cool bunk beds and we stayed up all night talking. In the morning Bridie took me home but my mum was nowhere to be seen. Tish sat me and Liam, down (Martin was only 18 months at this time) and told us mum's staying at Joe and Maisie's for a week. I knew it was bad. Dad came in from work that night very quietly and went straight to his room. Tish was making the dinner and looking after all of us as usual.

A week went by, and I was asking when is mum coming home? Dad would just say "soon, son". I could see the tears in his eyes. Another week went by. Dad worked six days a week, sometimes seven, but this particular day, a Sunday, Dad was off, and I said, I want to see mum.

Tish did not look so happy, but she agreed because of us kids. So, we got Martin in the pram and set off across the road to our old estate at Giles House. All the way there no one said a word. Not me, Dad, Liam or Tish.

Once there, there was no chance I was going in those stinky pissy lifts, so I ran up three flights of stairs and still beat the lift. I used to love doing that and scaring Tish and Liam when they got out of the lift. I did it 100 times, trying to make them laugh.

We walked along the balcony to Maisie and Joe's, who lived on the very end of the block. As we walked past their kitchen window, Joe and my mum was in the kitchen. I ran in and cuddled my mum. She smelt like a pub. Dad came in after me and mum shouted, "what are you doing here?

Tish called us all in the front room then the shouting started. Dad was crying, saying: "I want you to come home." "What about the kids? Mum asked. Dad called us all into the Kitchen. Tish had Martin in her arms. I remember clearly, Dad asked us all individually if we wanted Mum to come home. "Pete, do you want mum home? I said yes. "Liam do you want Mum to come home? Liam said, "yes."

Dad said to Tish: "Tish, do you want Mum home? Tish's answer was straight to the point: "Over my dead body. Not after what she has done to you and all us kids." Mum was equally direct in her response to what she had heard: "I'm not coming home anyway," as she took another swig from the vodka bottle.

Dad then left the flat and we saw him walking past the kitchen window, crying. A short while later we all heard screaming. It was Maisie and Joe's boys, Jason and Martin. Somehow Dad had managed to tie some rope to the Balcony and the other bit round his neck. As we ran out Dad had one foot over the Balcony when Jason, Martin, and our Liam managed to stop him just in time.

I was screaming by now and ran into mum crying. She never even flinched, just stayed there drinking her Vodka, never moved a muscle. By now Tish is crying and screaming at mum: "look what you made dad do you slag".

Joe got my dad and took him home while Tish gathered all us kids, up and took us home. When we got there, Joe had left a note saying he had popped down the Prince of Wales with my dad for a few pints. It was horrible to see. All I could picture in my head was my dad with a rope around his neck. I can still see that picture in my now, in my head, clear as the nose on my face.

All I kept doing was looking out of the window and saying to Tish, "When's dad coming home? All of a sudden there is a knock at the door and its dad, drunk as a skunk with bottles of coke and crisps for us. Joe was with him and he put dad straight to bed. Joe said he had had a good chat with dad and he was ok. When Joe had gone, we checked on dad, then we all snuggled up on the brown sofa bed. We stayed up all night in case we heard any noise from dad's room.

At 6am dad's alarm went off and Tish ran to check on dad. When she got there, dad was dressed and said he was going off to work. Tish made dad a cup of coffee and dad assured her he was ok and not to worry. As always Tish was great with us. She gave us the day off school and took us to the shops to take our minds off everything.

Chapter 5
How I discovered boxing.

The way my mum was acting, abusing and treating people was a chapter of my life, I was happy to forget. I was about to embark on another, one that would significantly change my life for the better. Liam was still taking me to the Fisher Downs Club but had now taken up Boxing. By this point I said to myself, 'I've had enough of being beaten up'. Boxing is so good for self-defence and discipline, and I thought it would take my mind off everything, so I decided I wanted to have a go.

As soon as I got home, I told Tish. And when dad got home from work, I asked if I can I go. He said, "course you can". I remember it was a Wednesday evening. Liam said, get your stuff ready we are going. Boxing shorts, t-shirt, trainers and a towel. Off we went to the Fisher Club. As I walked in for the first time it was noisy and smelt of sweat. People were skipping, bags were being punched, people sparring and was music pumping out.

Liam took me over to this man with a flat nose. His name was Steve (Hiser). "This is my little brother Pete," said Liam. Just looking at him scared the hell out of me, I wanted to cry. Steve put his hand out and said, "shake my hand, son. Do you fancy a go? I said yes, so Steve called out to one of the fighters, Paul Carr, who was hitting a bag. "Come here? said Steve. The gym went silent, you could hear a pin drop.

Steve said to me, "turn your chin to the side. Paul is going to hit you on the chin so close your eyes." I shut my eyes as tight as I could then I heard a massive bang. I think it was a bag being hit. I opened my eyes and Steve smiled and said, "you passed the test, welcome to the Fisher." He called all the lads over to shake my hand and all welcomed me, it felt like a family from the very start. The first six weeks I never threw a punch, just working the feet. Steve said the foundations start from the feet up, you can't build a house without groundwork. We went home after our first session that evening and straight away, I said to Liam, "shall we spar?

Liam agreed but we soon found we had a bit of a problem; we never had any gloves or a gumshield. Back in the '80s a lot of families on our estate never had much of anything so we had to improvise. This time was no different so what we did was roll up loads of little socks inside a pair of bigger football socks and put them on our hands. And for a gumshield, we used orange peel. We looked a right pair of Wallies, but we were kitted out now and the venue for our spar was the outside balcony. Not the biggest venue I fought in, but it was my debut!

That first spar was a pretty painful experience I can tell you. Liam was a bit older than me and a little more experienced and he did make me cry, but I just kept coming back for more. Liam did ask if I was ok but he also said, "you have to learn to take the punishment as well as dish it out."

That same night of my 'boxing debut' I remember Dad coming home with tears in his eyes and calling Tish to his room. Not long after, Tish came out looking very unhappy and told me and Liam that we have to pack up all mum's clothes.

I'll never forget it; Tish went to the hallway cupboard and brought out this massive dark green suitcase with gold buckles. It was so big you could get both me and Liam in it at the same time. Of course, I did not want my mum to go so all the time Tish kept filling up that case with my mum's clothes I would be taking them out while crying my eyes out. I was only eight at the time and never understood what was going on but Liam was 13 and Tish 15, so they could see more clearly the hurt my dad was going through and how Mum's behaviour was affecting us kids. So, they thought mum leaving was for the best.

After Tish explained we were all staying with dad I said to Tish, "will we still see her? Tish replied, "If she cares that much about us, she will come and visit us and take us out". Once mum's case was packed, we all went and sat downstairs while dad stayed up in his room.

As always Tish made sure we had our favourite hot chocolate and biscuits while Martin had his bottle. As we were sitting there laughing and joking the phone rang and before we had a chance to respond dad shouted down: "Leave it". It rang a few more times before ringing off. About five minutes later the phone rang again and dad answered: "Hello". The phone was in the hallway so all us kids sneaked up to the living room door. All we could hear was her screaming down the phone. She was so loud I thought she was in the hallway. Tish said, "She's pissed again. I'm glad she's not here taking it out on dad".

Then dad starts crying again and we heard him say, "what about the kids? As soon as dad said that Tish quickly made us all come away from the door and sat us back down. "You are too young to be hearing all this", said Tish. With that dad slammed the phone down and said, "Fucking bitch", before storming back into his bedroom and slamming the door after him. Tish left it for a few minutes then went in to see dad and make sure he was ok.

Tish eventually came out at around midnight. It had been a long day, but Tish explained that mum was coming to get her case and was moving out. I remember thinking to myself. "It's all happening again like the night we left Ireland and came to London. Was she taking me somewhere else, are we all leaving dad?

Just as I was thinking about what might happen dad came out of his room and called Tish into the kitchen. We all followed, and dad pulled some blue rope out of the draw. Only a few months before he had tried to kill himself with some blue rope, so I panicked straight away thinking, was this the same blue rope he had round his neck a while ago and was he going to try the same thing again?

My heart was in my mouth but then dad handed the rope to Tish and said, "I want you to tie this rope around the suitcase and hang it out of the window". We lived in a ground floor maisonette then and I said why don't we just wait for mum to knock on the door. But that's what dad wanted. He also insisted, "Make sure the case is high enough so she can't just grab it and run off. I want her to come in and tell you she's leaving". Thinking about it now, maybe it was some kind of message, dad was sending to mum about how he felt when he tried to end his life not long before.

By now it was getting late so Tish took me and Martin up to her room. I wanted us to stay in her room so she made up a bed for us on the brown fold up couch. She made sure we were snuggled in before going back downstairs to see dad. Martin fell asleep as soon as his head hit the pillow but I just lay there staring up at the ceiling. Tish had some of those glow stars all over the ceiling. They lit up in the dark and I used to like laying there and watching them. There was always one that stuck out and I remember staring at it and praying to it.

I used to say things like, "please God let us have a normal life like the one we had in Ireland". I only had good memories until we left that beautiful farmhouse and land to move to London. I'm now lying in bed crying once again, with tears rolling down my cheeks. Seems like I spent the whole day crying for one reason or another. It was getting on for 1am now and I was still awake when Tish comes in and tells me to go to sleep. I asked if dad was ok and she assured me he was fine. It had been a long day and it was not over yet because just as Tish gave me a kiss and a cuddle to say good night there is an almighty knock at the door.

Tish, startled by the noise, quickly jumped up to see what was going on when Liam came running into her room and shouting, "It's mum and she's drunk again and having a pop at dad". By now Martin had woken up because of all the commotion mum was making. Tish being Tish quickly went downstairs and made her presence felt. She told mum to keep the noise down as the kids were in bed and she was waking up half the estate. Mum as always was totally oblivious to everyone and everything around her. It was not long before she turned on Tish, shouting, "Shut your mouth or I'll slap you, you lying little bitch".

By now, Liam had climbed in bed with me and Martin and kept repeating, "She's drunk again, she's drunk again". Before I knew it, Tish reappeared and jumped in with us as well. Poor little Martin was crying. Tish was always our Rock and this time was no different. As she cuddled Martin in one arm and me in the other, she said, "Don't worry, it will be ok. She (mum) will have to go through me first to get to you".

29

Our Tish was like a human shield and would always take the brunt of the violence if it meant us kids had it a bit easier.

At that moment dad came into the bedroom and said, "Mum wants to speak to you all". Tish bundled us all towards the bedroom door. I still remember my mum standing there beside my dad. "Say something to them", dad shouted. "I don't want to be here anymore, I'm leaving," said Mum. By now I'm absolutely distraught and just shouted: "NO MUM", as Tish held me back in an effort to comfort me.

Dad said to mum, "Look, you're going to have to take the kids, how can I look after all of them on my own? I'm a good worker, please don't leave them like this?

Mum looked at me and said, "I'll take the two smallest, Pete and Martin. The other two are old enough to look after themselves". Dad, forever the diplomat and voice of reason turned to me and said, "do you want to go with your mum? "No, I want us all to stay together". I loved being with my brothers but Tish, by now was like a second Mum, a Human Shield and our Rock. There was no way I was going to be parted from her.

Tish was always there for all of us, dad included so it was no surprise when she unleashed years of anger after hearing what Mum had said about wanting to split us all up. Looking her up and down in total disgust, Tish shouted, "You horrible bitch, you don't deserve kids. The way you have treated us you're just a horrible, spiteful drunk. What woman beats their kids and take them away from their country and lovely home?

"We were happy then, just leave us alone. I'm not stupid, you left there because you couldn't keep yourself out of trouble. I know your leaving dad for someone else. You could have done that in Ireland. At least we would have had family there to help us".

True to form mum took a swing at Tish but dad had finally had enough. He had never laid a finger on mum before, but this time he pushed her back to protect Tish and us. And in no uncertain terms told her, "Don't you ever lay a finger on my kids again, enough is enough, get out of my house".

With that, dad told Tish and Liam to lower mum's suitcase from the balcony. I never knew at the time but it would be another 30 years before I ever set eyes on her again.

Chapter 6
Time to stick together.

As soon as the front door shut dad looked at us all and said, "now we all have to stick together". I can't remember exactly what the date was but I know it was Christmas week, 1986, a few days before my birthday. It was by far the longest day I can remember and one I definitely would rather forget. Although that was probably the longest and most exhaustive day of my young life so far, I was still up early. As dad said the night before, he was a good worker and had already left to earn money and put food on the table. Once Tish got up, I said to her: "Was last night a dream? Tish was always honest with us and just replied, "No, mum's gone now."

"Do you think she will come back for my birthday? I asked. Tish just replied, "I don't know. But whatever happens, dad will make sure your birthday is the best." Once Tish had said that I knew everything was going to be ok. After Mum left, me and Liam were spending pretty much all our time down at the Fisher. We would be boxing three days then playing football or swimming the rest of the time. For me and Liam, it was a place to go and relax and enjoy ourselves, but Tish was having to take on the role of mum to me and Martin. Tish was pretty much 'mum' to us anyway but now it was official.

Tish was still a kid, herself at just 15 years old, and looking after me and Martin, as well as running the home, meant she had no choice but to sacrifice her own childhood. And when she did find time to go out with her friends, she had us with her. The day of my birthday soon arrived, and I was super excited. I could not sleep all night and was wide awake when Tish came in to wish me a happy 9th birthday and to come downstairs and open my presents. As much as I was looking forward to opening my presents the best one, I got was seeing my dad standing there. For once he was not in his work clothes. He was dressed very smartly, nice shirt and trousers. I could not help but notice he had a bit of rope around his waist to keep his trousers up and wondered if it was the same rope that he tried to do himself in with a while ago at Giles House. Even now, all these years later, I still have flash backs when I am similar blue rope.

Dad was never one for giving out cuddles, but he did this day and when he said he was taking the day off for my birthday I just could not stop smiling. I was so happy I nearly forgot to open my presents. Dad handed my first present, a pair of black and white Title boxing boots in the Fisher colours. Dad got them two sizes too big on purpose so I would grow into them. Then I opened my second present, and it was a pair of red boxing gloves. I put them on and said to Tish, "What's that smell? "It's real leather, Pete, you're a real boxer now."

This was the best birthday ever and when dad asked if I would like to go to the Wimpy (fast food restaurant) for lunch I could not get dressed fast enough. Back in the 80's, where we came from, going to the Wimpy bar for Burger and Chips in Bermondsey was like having Tea and Cucumber sandwiches at the Ritz. You only ever went to places like that on special occasions.

I asked dad if me and Liam could go and have a spar to try out my new boots and gloves before we went to the Wimpy. There we were on the balcony with one boxing glove on each and an old sock, padded out. I was the boxer that day because I had the boots on so there was no way Liam was going to beat me. I think he let me win as it was my birthday.

Afterward, dad called us to get ready. I came down the stairs still wearing my boxing boots and gloves. Dad looked at me and half-heartedly said, "Take those gloves off, you can't walk down the High Street with those on". Then Tish looked at me even closer and said: "What's that on your face? I said, "I have your make up on." Tish said, "Boys don't wear makeup, take it off".

To cut a long story short I wanted to go out looking like a real boxer with all my gear on, so I used Tish's black eye liner to give me two black eyes and used her bright red lipstick on my nose to look like I had

33

been whacked a few times. I said it's my birthday and I can do what I want. Dad agreed.

Looking back on it I must have looked a right wally, but I had quite a few cars driving past and beeping so I must have given them a laugh, and it made me feel like a real boxer. Anyway, it beat being called a stupid little Leprechaun or a backward Irish bastard. And it was definitely better than taking beatings at school, and from my mum.

As soon as we got to the Wimpy, I took off my gloves and ordered a Bender (that's a Frankfurter in Wimpy language) in a Bun and chips. And for dessert, I had my favourite, an Ice Cream Float. I think I ate the lot in five minutes flat.

Us kids were having a great time, lots of nice food and then the birthday cake came out. Dad did us proud as usual and he was happy watching all of us enjoying ourselves, but he had tears in his eyes and knew he was missing mum. As I blew the candles out, I made a wish. Dad looked at me and smiled as if we both knew what I was wishing that Mum would come back. Dad just gazed at me and said, "Enjoying yourself, Son? I just stared back at him and said, "This is the best day, ever. Is Mum coming back tonight? Dad solemnly replied, "I hope so".

As we left the Wimpy, dad joked about how full up, we all were so no more food for a month. No matter how hard times were and how down my dad was he always found a way to make us laugh.

After we had been home for a few hours we heard the letterbox bang, just the once. It was around 7 pm when dad went to the door. "Is that Mum? I shouted. "No, there's no one here", said dad. Just before he closed the door, I could see a blue envelope on the door mat. Dad picked it up, saw who it was from, and handed it to me.

At that moment I felt like everything was in slow motion. Dad just walked off into his room. The card just said, 'To Pete from Mum'. That was it, nothing more. I turned to Tish and said, "Mum never came to see me on my birthday. That was the wish I made when I blew the candles out at the Wimpy".

34

Tish was always there to comfort me and said, "She's a horrible woman. I know I'm not your mum. I'm your sister but if anything is ever wrong you can tell me. That women don't deserve kids".

Tish never normally spoke like that to me. I knew she was living a dog's life but what she said to me really sunk in, and I realised that I no longer had a mum and may never see her again. It had been a long day and Tish said it was about time I went to bed. As I walked past Dad's room, I could hear him crying again.

Mum leaving, left a massive void in the coming weeks. My head was all over the place and I was having a tough time at school. Bermondsey was a close-knit community back then and news travelled fast, especially when it is bad. As soon as I got back to school, it did not take long for me to get back into the old routine of fighting. Pretty much everywhere I went someone was saying, 'Your mum's left you, you don't have a mum'.

I could not keep taking it so the only way to deal with it was to fight. By now I was learning how to hold my hands up and one day the fighting got out of hand. One particular lad had bullied me since I first came to the school, just because I was small, and I was Irish. After days of hearing about my mum leaving, I just snapped. He kept going on, saying thing like, 'your mum doesn't love you, that's why she left you'.

I got this lad in a headlock and threw him to the ground. Even though my Monkey boots were two sizes too big I just kept kicking him in the face until I knocked his two front teeth out. There was blood everywhere. Eventually, the Head Teacher dragged me off him and as she did so I shouted, "Your mum might not love you now, either. That's the last time you bully me".

With all the problems my dad was going through, me having problems at school was the last thing he needed. The Head Teacher must have thought it was serious because the Police were called. The Police said I needed help and to go and see someone. When I got home, Dad cried and said, "If you get in any more trouble, I could end up losing you."

When I explained that the other kid had bullied me since we came over from Ireland and that he kept saying mum never loved me, Dad did say the other kid deserved it, but the fighting had to stop. I still got grounded and was stopped from going to the boxing club for a while. Whenever dad got in from work, I would ask If I could go boxing but he kept saying no.

Liam was still going down the Fisher but what I did not know was Steve Hiser, the head coach kept asking where I was. Liam covered for me for about a week and then Steve eventually cornered Liam and asked, "What's happened to Peter, doesn't he fancy it anymore? Liam could not keep making excuses for me, so he told Steve that I had been grounded for fighting at school but never told him the full story.

Chapter 7
A lesson learned.

After a few weeks, dad decided I had been punished enough and lifted my curfew. The first thing I could think of is getting back down the Fisher and start boxing again. As I walked back into the gym for the first time in weeks the whole place went quiet, once again you could hear a pin drop, just like the first time I went to the gym. It was like one of those old Western films my dad used to watch on the tv when the lone gunman walked into the saloon bar to face the local gang. The music paused, lads dropped their skipping ropes and there were no more loud thuds from gloves slamming into punchbags.

"Hey McDonagh, where you been", Steve shouted. When Steve says something, you feel like you want to shit yourself, especially when you're a scrawny little nine-year-old like I was. He was around 5ft 8, had scars across both eyes and his nose was pushed right into his face. That was the main thing I noticed about him when I first met him. He looked like he had been cracked in the face with a sledgehammer. That was funny, really because the first thing Steve told me was that boxing is all about hitting and not getting hit. I think he saw me staring at his bugle when he said it because he quickly reasoned, "take no notice of my nose, I did that playing football". Could have bloody fooled me, unless of course he was playing against Mike Tyson.

After asking me why I had been away so long I sheepishly said, "I had been naughty". Of course, Steve knew why I had not been training because Liam had already caved in under pressure. "Get gloved up McDonagh, your sparring": Steve said, sternly. "But I have not been training and I got no gumshield", I argued. Steve was having none of it and told Sam and Jason to glove up (prepare to spar). I could not make out what was going on because not only had I not been training for a while, but I was a novice 9-year-old and Steve was telling me to get in there and spar with two 11-year-olds, who had more experience and had in fact had competitive Club bouts. I remember thinking, they are going to kill me. To confuse me even more while Jason was psyching himself up in the ring by punching his head, Steve was whispering in his ear and Jason was smiling.

As soon as the bell rang Jason marched all over me and battered me from one corner of the ring to another. The bell to end the round took longer than it took me to swim from my favourite rock to the Connemara shore. Steve was supervising from outside the ring and as soon as the bell rang, Steve abruptly shouts: 'JASON OUT', SAM, IN'. I complained to Steve that I was tired, but he just looked into my eyes and said: "Away you go". I had my head down and thought, "I don't need another round of this". Away I went again and this time it was Sam that was beating me from pillar to post. I felt blood streaming down my face and could see it on my shirt. I learned very quickly that when you're getting bashed up, a two-minute round seems to go on forever. I was relieved when Steve shouted: 'TIME'.

As I got out of the ring all battered and crying, Steve quickly explained to me why he put me through what he did. Looking at me with that stern 'Sledgehammer' face of his he said, "Son, if you ever bully anyone again you will never come back to my gym. We don't build bullies here; we build characters and champions. Never use boxing outside this gym. Now go home and think about whether you want to be a champion or a bully? As I walked out of the gym there were a few remarks about me being a bully but the thing I remember most is looking in the mirror and seeing blood trickling out of my nose and the start of a black eye, appearing. I also thought about how I was going to explain my injuries to Tish. One thing for sure was, I didn't have to borrow her make-up this time to look like a beaten-up boxer. I found out the hard way how to become one for real!

As soon as I opened the front door I came face to face with Tish. I could see the panic on her face as she said, "What happened to you, Pete? Once I had told her she said, "Right, you're not going back there". Funnily enough, I was thinking exactly the same thing. Word soon got around school that I was sparring the bigger kids that were featured regularly in the local paper, the Bermondsey News. After that people started talking to me differently and wanting to be my friend. It's funny how some people suddenly want to be your friend after you have been beaten black and blue! I went home that day and told Tish I'm going back down the Fisher. "You're not going boxing again," she said. "It's ok because I'm only going swimming", I insisted. So, what I did was put all my boxing gear in Liam's bag. By this time Liam was more interested in football so I had to plead with him to cover for me but not to tell Tish.

It was now two weeks since I had my arse handed to me by Sam and Jason so when I walked back into the gym Steve walked up and told me Liam had explained everything about why I was grounded, and why I did what I did. Steve put his arm around me and said, "Son, I'll tell you what, you got some heart to get through that spar the way you did. Look in the mirror and tell yourself, I'm not a bully, I'm going to become a champion and inspire others who have been bullied". As time went on, I think Steve took a bit of a shine to me. He knew about my schooling and life at home. In time, being at the Fisher Club was like one big family. We were a TEAM (Together Everyone Achieves More).

Chapter 8
Dad still battling his demons.

After a couple of weeks of telling Tish I was going swimming at the Fisher, I plucked up the courage to tell her the truth. I told her I had been going boxing all the time. She then admitted that she knew all along because Liam had told her. What she did say, though was, "I can see you are happy but never ever lie to me again".

Just to reassure her I explained that I could tell Steve anything and that all the lads are so friendly. Fisher was like a family and being in the gym was like being in a new home for five days a week.

I was now about 10 years old, and Martin was just about to celebrate his fourth birthday. Although it had been a couple of years since mum had left, dad was still struggling with her not being at home. Dad would regularly cry himself to sleep in his room with just a bottle of Whisky to keep him company.

Dad was a very hard-working man, and worked seven days a week just to make ends meet. Although Tish was still in her teens and sacrificing her childhood by bringing up us kids, dad was equally committed to our family unit by putting food on the table, clothing us and paying the bills. Unfortunately, working all the hours god sent was just not enough. Dad's bosses knew he had four kids to feed on his own so they helped him out as much as they could with a bit of cash in hand. But dad could still not manage to pay all the bills, so he claimed housing benefit as well.

One day we got a letter drop onto our mat. Dad could not read so Tish used to open all his mail. The letter was from the council saying that they had proof that he had been working cash in hand and that they were going to freeze his benefits and that he would have to pay any money back that he had claimed. I will never forget it; it was a Sunday. It was a beautiful day outside and very hot, but the atmosphere soon changed once Tish open that letter.

We knew dad was not coping so well but after hearing what Tish had read to him, he just looked at her dejectedly and said, "I can't do this anymore", and got up and walked out, slamming the front door behind him. The last time I saw dad that down and depressed was when he was heading out of Joe and Maisie's flat with the blue rope and trying to throw himself off the balcony.

I think Tish and Liam thought the same so we quickly got Martin ready and put him in his pushchair before rushing out of the door to chase after dad.

There was two or three different directions he could have gone when he rushed out but lucky for us, we managed to find him pretty quickly. We followed him from a distance so he could not spot us. Dad was walking up the Jamaica Road then turned off right in the direction of the river Thames, opposite the Tower of London. By now we were getting really worried, and we were right to be. As dad got closer to the river, Tish hurried us all up. We were just out of dad's sight now but we could just see him in the distance. It was starting to get dark now and it looked like dad was looking over the edge of the wall, and the drop into the Thames below.

Moments later dad started to climb the wall and we could see some kind of heavy weights tied to his shoes, by the laces. Tish immediately ran over to him, quickly followed by me while Liam stayed with Martin. Once we got there, dad was tying more weights to his shoes. It turned out they were engineering bricks, the ones with the three holes through them. As soon as dad realised, we were there he turned to Tish and said, "I can't do this anymore".

Tish, realising dad looked pretty serious about taking the plunge into the deep waters of the Thames weighted down by the engineering bricks, replied, "But dad, what about us? We got nobody. mum's gone, you can't leave us, please dad? "But Tish, I can't carry on I've had

41

enough. The woman I loved has left me for another man, I'm no good for nothing", he insisted.

"But dad, don't you love us, just look at Pete? said, Tish. Dad looked broken and was crying and just kept saying, "But I'm better off not here". By now, Liam had walked over with little Martin in his pushchair. Tish took Martin out of his pushchair and held him up to dad and said, "Dad you have a baby, please? We will not survive without you. Please get down from there and we will get the help you need I promise but let's just get you home, get a Whiskey and put the kids to bed. But if you don't love us then jump?

Thankfully, after looking at us all standing there in front of him, dad saw sense and climbed down. As we all cuddled dad, we all said how much we loved him. Dad just put his head in his hands before looking up at Tish and said, "I'm so sorry for putting you through this. I will never do anything like this again until Martin is 16 and he can look after himself".

We then all walked home, and Tish turned to Dad and said, "If you ever feel like this again, after work go and have a few pints in the pub. Just take some time on your own". The local pub near us was called the Prince of Wales. We could see the pub from our maisonette. That's where we could find dad if he had had a hard week. And at least when Dad rolled out pissed up at 11pm we could watch him stagger home safely. Regardless of how drunk he was, he would always return home with a bottle of coke and plenty of bags of crisps. I know getting drunk was not the answer to his problems but if it helped dad cope and keep the demons at bay that was good enough for us.

Chapter 9
Meeting my new best friend.

When I was not boxing, I was always kicking a football around. The other thing I was pretty good at was fixing or building BMX bikes. Back in the 80's BMX riding was all the rage and I suddenly found myself running my own little business. What I used to do was go rummaging around in skips looking for old BMX's and other old bike parts. And when I had everything, I needed I would make a bike up and sell it off. It was not long before I had enough parts and spares to open my own BMX shop. Everything was sold as seen of course.

Not every BMX sale, though went as planned. There was a subway near where we lived. It used to run under the Jamaica Road. You could pick up some serious speed under that subway, that's where we used to go to road test the bikes I had built. I used to make sure the brakes were working ok, that kind of thing. One day I was selling a bike to a kid, and he took it for a test ride. As he was picking up speed and flying down the subway the back wheel came flying off and he was gliding along on just the back forks as the detached wheel went rolling down the subway, just missing an old couple, carrying their shopping home. Lucky for me the kid on the bike was ok and the old couple never went home with a spare wheel in their shopping bag. The kid agreed to not say anything as long as I gave him the bike for free. I may have lost out on £2.50 but Peter's Wheels stayed open for business.

It was around this same time everyone used to wear Belcher chains. That was the trend in Bermondsey, anyway. A Belcher was a thick gold chain with the links. I would be lucky If I could afford a decent designer t-shirt so a Belcher chain was definitely out of the question. Dad was always one to try and help us fit in so if I could not have a Belcher chain, we decided the next best thing was a bicycle chain. Dad used to dip them in vinegar overnight and the next day they would be super shiny.

A few days after nearly taking out two OAPs with the runaway bicycle wheel I was out riding my BMX and minding my own business when, from out of nowhere, a kid came flying around the corner on a pair of roller skates and nearly crashed into me. In those days it was fashionable not to have any brakes on the bike so what we used to do was wedge one of our booted feet between the frame and the back wheel to slow the bike down. After I eventually managed to stop, I looked up at the kid and thought: 'He's not from around here'. After we got talking for a bit, he explained that he had just moved into the pub down the road. "Is that the Prince of Wales", I said. "Yes", he replied. My Dad had told me the Landlord had a son about my age and dad had told the Landlord about me as well. When I explained that my dad drinks there and likes a drop of Whiskey, and told him his name is Bill, the lad knew exactly who Dad was.

"My name's Pete, what's your name", I said. "Harry", He replied, "nice to meet you? You could tell Harry was not from around here because he was dressed from head to toe in designer gear. I can still remember how he looked, even after all these years. Harry was wearing a Naf jumper, Paisley Jeans, and had an earring in his left ear. It was the first time I had seen a boy wearing an earring. You have to remember back in the '80s there was the emergence of the boy bands like Wham and Bros, so wearing earrings was becoming a popular fashion statement with young men.

In contrast, I was the stereotypically rough and ready Bermondsey Boy. Looking me up and down Harry inquisitively asked, "What's that around your neck, is it a bicycle chain? I just sheepishly nodded and said it was "my chain". I asked Harry if I could have a go on his roller skates and he agreed. That was a bad idea because as soon as I put them on and stood up, I went arse overhead. That was the first and last time I ever put those skates on. By now we had made our way back home and as luck would have it the Ice Cream van had just pulled up outside our flats. Harry pulled out a five-pound note from his designer Paisley Jeans and said, "Fancy an Ice Cream?. Harry did not need to ask me twice. I was straight in there and asked for a Popi, which was an Ice

Cream with a red lolly on top. I was so happy about Harry getting me an Ice Cream I said I would make him up a bike, but he said, "I'm ok thanks, I already have a bike and a motor bike as well". I thought, 'bloody hell, this kid's rich'. While we were sitting there laughing and joking Martin appeared from the flats. I introduced Martin to Harry and Harry asked him how old he was. "I'm Five," Martin proudly replied. "I have a little brother as well, His name is Danny and he's five as well, would you like to meet him? Martin got all excited and said, "yes please". I told Harry we would have to go and ask Tish, first. "Is that your mum? asked Harry. "No, Tish is my sister. Our mum left us".

Looking at Harry's face I think he looked a bit shocked and surprised that our older sister was bringing us up. Anyway, Tish said it was fine for us to go and meet Danny at the pub as long as I held Martin's hand and we stayed together. So off we went to meet Danny at the pub opposite our flats. We had to walk through the pub bar to get upstairs. As we were walking up Harry shouted, "Mum, you there? All of a sudden, his Mum, Irene, appears and introduces us. "Mum this is Pete and Martin. These are Bill's boys; you know Bill who comes in the pub? After saying hello, Harry's mum calls Danny from his room to come and meet us and we all go downstairs to play pool in the bar. In case you're wondering how is it that four young kids were allowed to play pool in a saloon bar in mid-afternoon, this was the 80's when pubs had to close from 3pm until 5.30pm. If I remember it was a few years before all day opening of pubs was introduced.

We were having such a good time in the pub that Tish had to come over and remind us of the time and that our tea was ready. Thinking about it know it sounds funny. Can you imagine your teenage sister marching into a pub to drag her 11- and five-year-old brothers out of the pub at 5pm in the afternoon? Social Services might have something to say about that now…

Anyone looking in from the outside probably thought me and Harry were an odd match-up and we did move around in different worlds but as soon as we shook hands for the first time, we became the best of friends. Wherever I went, Harry went and vice versa. The same went for Martin and Danny. We were always taking it in turns to have sleep overs. In fact, Irene became more like a step mum, over time. Liam was

45

that much older and had his own friends and at last, Tish was able to get out more and enjoy some time with people her own age. My dad used to drink with Harry's dad, Alan and life was slowly becoming more relaxed for everyone.

Harry was a member of the Lynn Boxing Club a couple of miles away. I tried to get him to come over to the Fisher, but he was happy where he was. And because we went to different schools we could only really meet up at weekends If I was not at a boxing show.

Chapter 10
My first bout

Meeting Harry and his family that summer of 1988 was a pretty significant time in my life back then. It also coincided with me moving up to secondary school. The only good thing about going to a new school was it was literally over the road from our house, so I could roll out of bed and into the classroom. Apart from that, it was the same old story of being picked on but not quite as bad. I was still pretty small for my age, but the other kids seemed massive to me. A few of them tried their luck as the word went around that I was going to be having my first carded boxing bout at the end of the week, so I was pretty much left alone.

Any boxer will know this, but if you have never boxed before I'm going to let you into a little secret. Of course, you need to learn how to throw various punches and use your footwork to position yourself and be able to move quickly. But the main thing for most boxers is to try and understand how to get their diet right. Some boxers are really good and very disciplined but not as many as you may think. I had not even had my first bout yet, but I was already thinking, "I'd rather have a belly than starve".

Steve always made a point of saying, "you have to watch your weight otherwise you will always be fighting above your natural weight". Did I bloody listen? No, I bloody did not! It was too late now anyway; it was Saturday, and my big day was here, I was now 11 years old. Me and Liam went off to the Fisher to meet the other lads. Steve soon turned up with the club van and we all piled in. The first thing Steve says is, "everyone done their weight".

Of course, everyone says, "yes". I'm sitting in the front of the van and Steve turns to me and says, "McDonagh, have you done your weight? I replied, "All I have had is two packets of crisps and a Mars bar." "That's no bloody good for your first fight", said Steve. Me being me cheekily said, "I saw an advert on tv saying a Mars a day helps you work rest and play".

The other lads had a good laugh about my response but I don't think Steve was too happy. That said we always had a good laugh in the van on the way to shows. My amateur debut bout was against the St Marys Club in Strood, Kent. As we pulled up at the venue, you could hear a pin drop. Steve must have loved that moment because it was the only time any of us kids were quiet.

As soon as we entered the building Steve went straight up to the booking table to give in our medical cards. The weigh in scale was right next to the table and in turn, each one of us got on the scale. I knew that I had to weigh in no more than 42kgs but those two packets of crisps and Mars bar must have tipped me over the edge because I weighed in at 44kgs. I remember Steve looking down with his reading glasses on and seeing I was 2kgs over. To say he was very unhappy is an understatement.

Once everyone had weighed in, we had to wait to see if we were fighting or not. That's when we all look around to see if anyone looks around the same size and weight. So, we would look each other up and down. There would also be a few spare boxers around in case they were needed. While we were waiting around Steve would be matching up the weights, ages and bout experience with the other coaches to see who he could match us with.

When Steve came back, he would sit us all down and we would all be biting our nails in suspense, waiting to find out if we made the bout sheet. Before I knew it, Steve belted out, "McDonagh, you're on, get gloved up". Steve named some of the other lads and they too were told to get ready. When some of the other lads could not get matched up for whatever reason, you could see the relief on their faces. At that particular moment, I was thinking, "wish I was them". Then there were the lads that came along as spares not thinking they would be matched. You could see the colour drain from their faces. Five minutes earlier they were shadow boxing and saying how much they wanted to fight. It is funny how people's moods can change so quickly. I was always amazed why us boxers put ourselves through such trauma.

Because of my age, my weight and being a junior, I was the first bout of the night. I was so nervous I did not know what to do. I must have gone to the toilet about 20 times before the bout. My belly was doing somersaults. I swear if I had lived around the corner I would have been straight out of that door and home. Let me tell you, anyone, that says they do not get nervous before going out and boxing in front of hundreds of people is either a liar or as mad as a box of frogs. I suppose that's where the saying, 'fight or flight', comes from.

Before any bout amateur or pro, you have to see the doctor for a medical to make sure your fit enough to box. They check everything, blood pressure, heart rate, etc. The last thing the doc checks is your hands and knuckles. After about five minutes the doctor passes me fit and I'm ready to go. I must admit I did come close to telling the doc my hands were sore. Before I could say anything, Steve came in and said, McDonagh, get ready, you're on in half an hour. The doctor must have seen I was nervous because he asked if, 'this was my first fight'. I said thank you to the doc and he wished me good luck.

There was no going back now. As I was warming up a man came up and said 'McDonagh, Fisher, red corner'. My mouth was dry as a bone and to say I was nervous was an understatement. Steve gave me a drink of water and said we had 10 minutes to go so let's get your gloves on. I was fighting a kid from St Marys, the home club. The place was filling up now and I could hear people shouting and drinking in the hall next door. Steve gets the pads out and gets me warmed up. I'm not joking there was no power in my punches at all. It felt nothing like sparring.

The time came to make my amateur debut. The other lads from Fisher knew what it was like to have your first bout and were all there in the dressing room to give me support and cuddled me before I went out.

I was fighting a kid called Paul Merter and as I walked to the ring quite a few of his home supporters were shouting, 'come on Paul, knock him out'. What I remembered most was the smoke under the ring lights and the smell of lager. I got to the ring and walked up the three steps, through the ropes and onto the battlefield. Then the home boxer comes out and the crowd went absolutely bonkers. I thought my eardrums were going to burst. Steve, ever the calming influence, said, "forget the crowd, they can't help him in there, it's just you and him when the bell goes".

Steve insisted I face him and jog on the spot. Then the referee calls us together and I turn around and saw my opponent. He looked bloody massive compared to me. It was at that moment I realised why eating crisps and Mars bars was not a good diet for a boxer. Steve wished me good luck; butterflies were still buzzing around in my belly.

As soon as the bell went the butterflies disappeared and I was focused on my opponent. Before I knew it the three, two-minute rounds were over, and the referee had grabbed both of us by the arm and we were waiting for the judges to announce the decision. The fight was close but I was just glad it was over. Steve was smiling at me so that was a good sign. As he was taking my gloves off, Steve said 'well done, son'. The fight was close but we are fighting on the other boy's show so it might go his way'.

It was a majority decision, which means two judges scored for one boxer and one for the other. Sure, enough my opponent, Paul Merter got the decision but I knew that day that I wanted to be a boxer and I was now a real member of the Fisher Boxing Club. The real bonus for us kids after we boxed was that we got a meal ticket whether we won or lost.

We had fun on the way home in the van and everyone was very supportive. I was the last one to be dropped off and Steve walked me up to my door. Tish and my dad excitedly rushed to open the door and Tish said: "how did you get on? "I lost". Steve, who was directly behind me interrupted and said, "He's learned you only lose if you give up". Steve then said to my dad, "you should be proud of your son, he boxed really well and it was very close". Dad was very appreciative and said: "Thanks Steve, this means a lot".

I could not sleep that night I was still buzzing from the fight. I was laying there thinking. I have done it. I could not wait to go back to the boxing gym and to school to tell my friends.

When I got back to school on Monday, my friends asked how I got on in my first bout. I told them I had lost but it was a close fight. At the end of the week the local paper (South London Press) came out and there was a picture and a report about me in it. The reporter said I put up a 'Gutsy Performance' I must have shown that report to everyone in South London, and half of Ireland as well. I was back in the gym as well the same week and Steve warned me again about my diet, but I could still not help stopping off at the chippy and the sweet shop after training.

I had my second bout two weeks later and lost another bout on a majority decision. I was giving too much weight away and Steve once again warned me about my diet. In fact, it was getting so bad that the lads at the gym started calling me the Chip Shop Kid. My weight and diet were so bad, before, I knew it, I had lost seven bouts in a row. I was just too fat and was giving away height and reach as well. So, Steve sat me down and said, "Look, if you're not listening to me, you might as well give up or go to another club. No more 'chip shop kid'. We are going to Jersey in six weeks' time. If you prove to me, you want to go then you will have to get the weight off. I can get you a fight at 40kgs".

I was getting stick at school as well because I had had seven bouts and lost seven and the other kids were calling me a loser. My confidence was at rock bottom. My best mate, Harry said, "you sure you want to carry on." Even my family was saying," you sure boxing is for you?

Chapter 11
No longer a loser

I still loved boxing, but I could not keep losing so I listened to Steve and stayed out of the chip shop. I also knocked the chocolate on the head as well. Steve started to check my weight every week and after a couple of weeks, Steve said, "McDonagh, your weight is coming down and you're training hard, well done. Bring your passport in tomorrow". I said passport, what's that? Steve said, "it's what you need to go on a plane".

I went home and told Tish that I needed a passport. Tish asked what I needed it for, so I told her I was fighting in Jersey and I'm going on a plane. Tish arranged it with dad to visit to the Irish Embassy and apply for a passport. When I told the kids at school I was going to fight in Jersey, they all started taking the piss, saying it was a long way to go to lose again. I said, "not this time. I have been training really hard and watching my diet".

Just my luck, Easter was coming up and I was fighting in a few days. I had a few easter eggs piled up at home but they would have to wait until I got back. The day finally arrived when we were going to Jersey. I had never been to an airport before or on a plane so it was a completely new adventure for me.

I made my way down to the Fisher and we all piled into the van and off we went to Gatwick Airport. I was so excited to be going but I could not get it out of my head that people thought I was a loser. There was real pressure on me to win.

A few hours later we had arrived in Jersey and were in our hotel. Steve quickly got us all sorted out with rooms and said, "right lads get to your rooms and get some sleep we have a big day tomorrow".

The next day we were decked out in the black and white of the Fisher colours. I managed to get hold of a programme to see who everyone had been matched against. I looked down the list and saw I was to box the son of the trainer, who was coaching the Jersey team. He had won two out of two so the odds of me getting a decision here did not look good, on paper at least. Once we got to the weigh-in this lad comes up to me and says, "I'm going to knock you out". Steve heard what the lad had said and just looked at me and said, "don't worry about it, talk is cheap". I looked at Steve and thought, 'talk is cheap, it's easy for you to say. You will be on the other side of the ropes when the bell rings.' I had forgotten that Steve was an amateur and a professional boxer.

Our bout was a special feature junior bout so we were due to be on last. We were boxing on a dinner show. There were lots of tables and what looked like some old school villains from London. Steve knew a few of them as he had been a trainer at the Fisher for what seemed like a lifetime. Steve had even trained the undisputed world welterweight champion, Lloyd Honeyghan. While we were making our way to the ring a few of the old school villains gave me a few cheers and shouted, 'come on you Bermondsey Boy'. Those old boys encouraging me filled me with a lot of confidence.

Once the bell rang my opponent flew from his corner and hit me with everything he had. The opening round was so one sided the referee took a close look at me a couple of times. In amateur boxing, it does not take much for the referee to step in and stop a contest if one of the boxers is on the wrong side of a beating. Eventually, the bell rang to end the round. As soon as I got back to the corner Steve looked at me with tears streaming down my face and said, "McDonagh, listen to me, what are you crying for? You're a Bermondsey boy, do you want to win this? I said, "yes Steve but he's strong," and he said," Listen, bite down on that gumshield and keep your hands high. All I want you to do is throw that jab as he comes in, ok? nothing else."

As the bell rang for round two I did exactly what Steve said. I just kept throwing the jab and the lad just kept walking onto it and I won the round clearly. When I got back to the corner Steve said, "how do you feel? Now listen you can win this fight". By now I'm smiling and said," I'm gonna win this fight". Steve says, "Right, now after you throw the jab, throw a straight right hand and move your feet. He will walk onto your punches again. You have turned the fight around now, so go and get him".

By now the crowd is cheering and I can hear my name being shouted. The bell rings for the third and final round and Steve gees me up for the final two minutes. All I can hear now is the crowd cheering, 'Come on Bermondsey boy'. Again, the lad comes out like a Bull in a China shop. I can only imagine his trainer/Dad had told him that there was no way he could lose to a kid that had lost seven fights in a row.

Just like the round before, as the kid comes in, he walks onto my jab and I follow it up with a right hand and that stopped him in his tracks. Then I started throwing three and four punch combinations and everything just came together. Everything Steve taught me in the gym was now coming together. Then the bell rang to finish the fight and I had this really funny feeling. It was a winning feeling is all I know how to describe it.

That kid looked like I did when I put Tish's make up on for my birthday party at the Wimpy bar a few years earlier. I walked back to my corner and Steve had a beaming smile on his face as if he had just won the world title. He cuddled me and said, "you got this one, son. I hope we don't get tucked up"

Until the referee held up my hand, I was still a loser. As we stood in the middle of the ring the announcer said, "and the winner by unanimous decision from, London, England, McDonagh" I just sunk to my feet and felt so relieved that, at last, after seven straight defeats I was now a winner. I had cried a lot in my young life up to that point and pretty much all because I was upset or sad but this time, I was crying tears of joy. The crowd must have enjoyed it because all of a sudden money came flying in the ring. When that happens, they call it Nobbins. Basically, for those non boxing people reading this it means that if the crowd liked the bout, they threw money into the ring for the two boxers to share out.

I was relieved when I got back to the dressing room. All those people that we're laughing at me and calling me a loser had no reason to anymore. Steve was so pleased he even said I could celebrate with a portion of chips. I did not need telling twice.

I was so proud I could not wait until I got home to tell dad and the rest of the family. "They will be so proud of you, son, you boxed brilliantly", said Steve. "You showed what you're made of. Keep up the hard work and you will become a champion one day".

We had a bit of a party that night in the hotel. There was plenty of Jersey chips, chocolate and bottles of coke. We knew how to celebrate us Fisher boys. We had such a late night I could hardly keep my eyes open on the flight home.

Chapter 12

At last I'm a winner

That morning as the Plane touched down, I was walking on air and as Steve dropped us all home in the van he said, as mine was the best fight of the night he would drop me off first.

I was used to being dropped off last, so I considered it a privilege to be the first out of the van. As I got out Steve said to the other lads, "three cheers for McDonagh" As I said The Fisher was like a second family. Everyone was slapping me on the back when I got out of the van and shouting 'see you on Monday'. I ran straight up the stairs of the flats and banged loudly on the front door. Tish answered and immediately said," did you win? And in my saddest voice I said," no, I have had enough". Tish cuddled me, and Liam and dad tried consoling me. I could not keep a straight face for much longer and dug deep in my bag to bring out my trophy. "What does that say, Tish? As Tish read 'WINNER' on the trophy she started crying and saying to dad, "he won". Everyone jumped for joy and Martin was parading the trophy around like the FA cup until the lid came off and all this money fell out.

There was about £45 in all and dad said, "where did you get all that money? I said it was such a good fight that the crowd through all this money in. I went through the entire fight again round by round and punch for punch. By the time I had finished exaggerating it a bit, it sounded like I was describing a Rocky film.

Once I had finished telling my 'Rocky' story Tish asked if I was hungry. After weeks of jacket potatoes and salad, I was happy to tuck into my favourite, fish fingers, chips and beans. Dad said, "what are you going to do with the money? Up until now I always wore my football shorts for boxing so I decided I was going to buy some proper boxing shorts in the colours of the Fisher and have my initials on them.

I did like my football shorts and I would always wear them when me and Liam played football on the green. Liam was a goalkeeper and I just used to take shots at him all day. Every now and again we would play one on one. I only liked that when it was raining or muddy because I could dive in the puddles and get really dirty. Tish used to go mad because she was the one doing all the washing.

One day Harry was round and we were playing football as usual. I used to take my winners' cup everywhere. For at least a month, wherever I went I took the trophy. Harry noticed it by the side of the goal post. He said," did you win the fight? Looking a bit down I said, "no". Just as he was about to say how unlucky I was he saw 'WINNER' in big letters on the trophy and called me a cheeky little Leprechaun. Harry suggested we go and show the trophy to his mum and dad so I run indoors to change my clothes. Tish, like a typical 'mum', shouted," what have you been doing, your filthy". I said I had been playing football outside and that I was going with Harry to the pub to show his mum my winners' trophy. Tish just held her hands up to her face and said," I'm sure you just roll around in puddles and mud all day for the fun of it". She was right there.

Quick as a flash I had changed my clothes and borrowed a bit of my dad's Old Spice aftershave and hair gel and I was away on my BMX. I still had muddy knees but as long as my hair was spiked up, I was good to go. I put the trophy in my bag and Tish said, "you will break that the way you are going". That trophy was more valuable than the Crown Jewels as far as I was concerned, no way was that happening.

When we got to the pub Harry's mum, Irene was working behind the bar. Harry shouted over," Mum guess what, Pete won his fight." Irene then walked to the end of the bar where Harry's Dad, was sitting with a group of friends and said," Alan, Pete won his fight in Jersey". Alan, who always liked his boxing, called me over and said 'well done, son' Then Alan and his mates, all gave me £5 each. I ended up with about £25 in all. I went and bought myself a pair of boxing boots with the money.

The day got even better when Irene said that once the other barmaid came in, she would take me, Harry, Martin and Danny to the Wimpy bar to celebrate. Then afterward, if it was ok with my dad, we could all have a sleepover at the pub. Irene and Alan were like second parents to me and Martin. The Prince of Wales was like a proper early 90's live music pub. There were some real characters there and if you needed any work done in your house there was always someone in there who could help you. And like most pubs in the cities around the country, there were the shady ones as well. But it was a great pub and there was never any trouble. Alan and Irene were very well-respected landlords. Harry had an older brother as well. His name was John and he had moved out with his girlfriend but used to pop home quite a bit to see his mum and dad. Every time he came in, he would see me, laugh and say, "have you moved in yet? Even my dad, if he was not working, would spend a lot of time in the pub.

Us kids would be upstairs on a Sunday tucking into a roast dinner while dad was downstairs having a drink and eating a roast, Irene had cooked for him. Dad was not a massive drinker, just a steady few pints. It was mainly to get him out of the house. Bermondsey was a great Community to live in and dad was very respected for the way he had to bring up four kids on his own. Every year Alan and Irene used to make up yearly awards and every year without fail dad would get the award for Best dad.

It was now two weeks since I won my first fight in Jersey and the Easter holidays were just finishing. I hardly ever looked forward to going to school but I was this time because I was going back as a winner and I could not wait to tell all my mates. So, with my trophy in one hand and a copy of the South London Press in the other, I arrived at school. If the kids at school did not believe me, I would show them the half page report about me winning my first bout and a picture of the referee holding my hand up in victory. The headline of that article read, 'Never Give Up'.

Life can be a funny thing. Home life was better and I was enjoying my boxing. It was also nice to hear the word 'well done' instead of 'unlucky'. I love sport but when it came to other subjects in school I was not interested. Unless it was a double period of PE on a Friday or break time, I was not interested. Thinking about it now, I was a pain in the arse for most of the teachers because although I wasn't nasty in any way I just never stopped talking and was a disruption. Unless it was PE or Art, I used to disrupt classes mainly to get kicked out of lessons. I did not realise it at the time but the real reason I could not get along at school was that I found it difficult to understand things. When I was younger, I thought my difficulty in learning things was because I never had a mum. Silly I know but, in those days, there was not the help available there is today for children struggling to retain information at school. I have since worked out that I could well be Dyslexic, which means difficulty in reading, writing and spelling.

Chapter 13

Bermondsey Boy

Another good friend of mine growing up was a lad called Frazier, who was a massive football fan. Frazier followed Millwall with a passion. By now I'm around 13 years old. Frazier was a year younger than me and when I was not boxing at the weekend, we would get down the Den (Millwall's ground) and cheer on 'The Lions'. Apart from reaching the FA cup final in 2004, Millwall have never really been a force to be reckoned with on the field but on the terraces, a portion of the fan base known as the 'Millwall Bushwhackers', were among the most ferocious in the country. Whenever Millwall played, whether at home or away, there was always a massive police presence, especially when we played West Ham.

Frazier's Dad was also a massive Millwall fan, so we used to go to the games with him. And as Frazier's Dad was friendly with quite a few of the Bushwhackers firm we got to know them as well. We would all meet in the Foresters pub on Blue Anchor Lane before and after the game. Me and Frazier would normally have a shandy but every now and again some of the younger Bushwhackers would slip us a few beers on the quiet. Then we would walk up to the ground and there were riot police on horseback, everywhere. There were always bottles and anything fans could get their hands on, flying through the air, either being aimed at the police or rival fans. You have to remember this was the late 80's, early 90's and football hooliganism was still very much in its prime.

As young and impressionable 13-year-old's, me and Frazier were mesmerised by what was going on and I have to be honest, it was a real buzz. Because I was so easily influenced, going to Millwall was starting to come between me and my boxing. I did have the odd bout here and there, but I was now starting to get older and getting more and more involved in the 'Bermondsey Boy' lifestyle, so boxing was becoming lesser and less of a priority for me. My Saturdays were now consisting of starting off with Jellied Eels and Pie and Mash followed by the pub and cheering on the mighty Millwall.

Life was difficult for us younger lads growing up in Bermondsey and even more difficult to find a nine to five, Monday to Friday job. We never had much chance of building up a CV, we were much more likely to be amassing a charge sheet. When people from our community went into a Bank or Post Office, they were not there to top up their bank book or cash a postal order, they were more likely to stick a gun up to someone's nose and make an unofficial withdrawal. There was a lot of armed robberies in banks back then, and cash in transit raids. Of course, no one condoned it but as long as no one was getting hurt it was pretty much accepted as a sign of the times.

By now, Steve was starting to notice that I was drifting in and out of the gym. Steve was not just a boxing coach to all the lads he was like a father/mentor and social worker all rolled into one. He sat me down one day and said, "Son, you don't box much now, if you're not careful you could end up going down the wrong road". Even my dad was going on at me to get back and focus on boxing. I did go back to boxing for a while. I was 14 by now and entered the Schoolboy Championship but just lost interest again. I was not putting in a hundred percent and started going on the missing list far too often. If something better came up boxing just got pushed onto the backburner.

To his credit, Steve tried his level best to keep me on the straight and narrow and away from all the bad influences that so many people in our local community had fallen victim to. At the Fisher, the walls are aligned with pictures of all our national amateur champions and all the pros that have won titles including undisputed world welterweight champion Lloyd Honeyghan, who, as I mentioned, Steve coached at the Fisher. I remember on one rare occasion I did manage to get to the gym, Steve said to all of us boys, "look at the wall, if you win a national title you go on the wall." Then he pointed to the picture of Lloyd and explained how he went over to the US and against all the odds, knocked out pound for pound No.1 boxer Don Curry to become world welterweight champion. And whilst Steve was quick to praise what could be achieved with hard work and dedication, he also made it clear by pointing out what could happen if we chose the wrong path.

Pointing to a particular picture on the wall Steve said," see him? What a great fighter he was. But do you know what he's doing now? He's doing life behind bars because he got caught up in the wrong life. He had the whole world at his feet. You have seen what Lloyd did. He was the first one in the gym and the last one out every night. It is possible for you to do what Lloyd did but if you don't put the work in you don't deserve to dream". Steve was one of the few people I listened to, but at age 14 I thought I knew it all. School was becoming harder and harder and although Tish thought I was trotting off to school every day I was giving it a swerve in favour of messing about on the Thames at Butlers Wharf, opposite The Tower of London. We used to go and play on barges that were moored by the old warehouses. One particular Friday at Butlers Wharf I was with my mate John Duligan. He was the kid I stayed with the night when it all came out about my Mum at my uncle's wedding.

We were messing about throwing boulders in the water trying to make big splashes. We found a massive boulder. It was very heavy; it took two of us to get it up on the wall. I said to John, "watch this splash", but as I leaned over to push it off the wall, I went over with it. For the life of me, I cannot work out to this day why I never let go of that boulder. All I know is I could feel my knuckles touch the bottom of the Thames. As I came up to the surface John panicked and said, 'I'm going to get help'. Even though I was in a bit of bother I was even more scared of what Tish was going to say if she found out. So, before I could tell him not to, he had gone off to get help. By the time he had got back, I was taking my blazer and shirt off and wringing them out. Funny thing was John had nipped into the Old Justice pub over the road and brought back an old fella that was pissed as a fart. If he had jumped in, I think I would have had to rescue him. I thanked him for coming out and he wobbled back into the pub.

I turned to John and said, "Tish is going to kill me." John just said, 'tell her you fell in a puddle'. "she's not bloody stupid," I argued. By the time

I got home, I was still soaking and smelling of the Thames. I did try and sneak in but Tish caught me and shouted, "what happened to you? I told her I fell over in a puddle and she looked at me and shouted," oh, so you fell in a bloody swimming pool in Bermondsey, did you? "You have not been to school have you, now how did you get that wet?

I decided to tell her the truth, that I fell in the Thames. Tish is like a dog with a bone when she gets going and I was not going to get one over on her. She asked who I was with but there was no way I was going to grass John, up. Tish told me in no uncertain terms that I was going to school on Monday and if I didn't, she would tell dad. So, I agreed. I went back to school for another couple of weeks but I was just not happy. Whether it was because I was getting frustrated because I was finding it difficult to understand things, I do not know why but I hated it. So, it was not long before I started making trouble, getting into fights, and letting off the fire alarms. I was just getting right out of hand and uncontrollable so the school soon called in my dad.

My behaviour was getting so bizarre the head teacher told dad, she thought I was sniffing glue and that I had crazy eyes. After everything dad had been going through over the years with Mum and looking after us four kids, this was the last thing he needed. Dad just broke down and started crying. "Dad", I said, "They are lying. I have been setting off fire alarms, fighting and not going to school but I would never sniff glue. I would never lie to you I promise." Dad knew I was telling the truth and said as much. He turned to the Head Teacher, sister Ann and said, "Pete may not be no saint but he's no glue sniffer. I'm taking him out of this school".

After we got home, we got a phone call from one of the teachers that I got on well with." I have heard about the report Mr. McDonagh and one thing I know is, Pete is not a glue sniffer. I know of a Centre in Peckham that I think will be good for Peter. It is more one to one" The place was more like a prison but I did learn more there in six months than I did throughout of all my schooling life. If you sat quietly for an hour, you could play pool for the rest of the day. It was more one to one and we did do a bit of work. After six months I told Dad that I did not want to go back and he said, "well what are you going to do then? I said I was going to get a job but Tish, the wise one as usual, said,
63

"your too young, go back boxing, it's the only thing you're happy doing and Steve is the only one that you listen to and has control of you".

Chapter 14
Getting stabbed

Whenever I lost my way, boxing was the only thing in my life that gave me a bit of structure and a massive part of that structure was Steve. We used to get all kinds of characters in the gym and a few of them were always in and out of jail for either drug dealing, shootings, or robbery. On the outside some of the lads were out of control but they all had the highest respect for Steve. He was like a father figure to us all. Steve would drop me off home some nights and never said much to us about his own family. We were his family but one night while he was dropping me home, he said," I don't know how Sandra(wife) puts up with me. I'm sometimes out seven nights a week, five in the gym and then shows at the weekend. I've hardly seen my girls grow up. Make sure when you have kids of your own you are there for them". I tried to lighten the mood a bit by saying," they probably love it that you're out of the house". Not sure how that went down, really, but Steve did have a little smirk on his face.

When a kid turns 15 any parent will tell you that they can become a bloody nightmare and I was no exception. I was starting to skip the gym even more now and drifting into petty crime, the exact thing Steve had always tried to steer us kids away from. It was nothing too serious, just things like stealing motorbikes and breaking into the beer factory at Chambers Wharf, just up the river from where I fell into the Thames a year or so before. Next door to the Holsten Pills factory we used to break into, was a gold bullion depot. We used to sit on the wall swigging beer and watching all the vans going in and out. Every time we saw those armour plated transits coming out, we would say to each other 'imagine taking out just one of those vans, we would be made for life'. We soon came back down to earth, though when we asked the older boys how much porridge we would get if we got caught. I will never forget it, one lad said, 'if you get caught blagging one of those vans you're looking at about twenty-five years behind the door'. It's one thing robbing a few bottles of beer and the odd moped but Gold bullion raids was a completely different league. It did not take a genius to work out, robbing cash transits vans was not a good career move and it was never an option, anyway. It was only ever just a few silly young kids' day dreaming because we had nothing else better to do. Once I came back down to planet earth I started to get back down to the Den and cheer on the Millwall. I will never forget one particular evening game on a cold Wednesday night.

For some reason, I had been separated from my mates. I was happily minding my own business walking over St James Bridge with a few cans of lager when these lads come walking towards me. As they moved parallel with me, I heard one of them say, 'hit him'. As one of them threw a punch I slipped it and put him on his arse with a peach of a right hand. Once he got up, he ran off but the other two were still game. As I was fighting one the other one walked behind me. The first one I had in a headlock and we were rolling around on the ground. All of a sudden, I felt a sharp pain in my leg but carried on fighting. Then his mate shouted, "I've stabbed him, let's get out of here".

I let the lad go and all I could see was blood everywhere. I quickly wrapped my Millwall scarf around the top of my leg to try and stop the bleeding. As I did this a man came up and asked if I was ok? I said, "quick get an ambulance". The man looked down at my leg and tied the scarf even tighter to reduce the loss of blood. Across the road, someone was coming out of a shop and the man helping shouted to, 'get an ambulance'. This night was turning out to be my worst nightmare, Millwall was playing at home, and first on the scene was the police. The first thing they said was, 'who you been fighting with? As there was no knife on the scene, I said I did it climbing over some railings and caught my leg on a spike. They asked what railings I got caught on and I just said, 'no comment, just get me an ambulance'.

The Police followed me to St Thomas' Hospital. As the Doctor was stitching me up, I stuck to my story that I had got impaled on some railings. The Doctor took one look at me and said sarcastically, "sure you 'got caught on railings, looks like a stab wound to me". I just looked at him straight in the eye and replied." I did it on some railings, no more questions. If I had been stabbed, I would have told you I had been stabbed." All of a sudden Tish rushed in all concerned and shouting, "what happened, are you ok? Now, I really did appreciate what the doctor did for me but he just would not let go and proceeded to tell Tish that I had said I did it climbing over railings but that in his 'professional opinion' I had been stabbed. Tish, always looked out for me and this occasion was no different. Tish told the Doctor and the Police," Pete's always climbing up and down trees, fences and walls. He's like bloody Spiderman". Luckily, they believed her and we could go home. I certainly did not fancy spending the night in the Police station.

The result of that stabbing was 16 stitches, six inside and 10 outside just under my bum. I could not sit down for two weeks. This is the first time I have ever told anyone this. I always told everyone including my family I got the injury on the railings. My luck was starting to run out now because not long after the stabbing I had the police on my tail again. Me and Harry decided to borrow his dad's motorbike and got caught riding down Jamaica Road with no helmets on and no insurance. They chased us all the way home. Me and Harry split up and they caught me as I was running up the stairs to the flats. The police threw me to the floor and slapped on the handcuffs.

'Where do you live', one of the policemen, asked. I said I live up at number 19. The police were not used to people telling the truth, they thought I was winding them up. When they got to my door, dad answered and the policeman said, "is this your son", dad replied, "Yes, it is". By this time the police had got the full story, had nabbed Harry and found out we had taken his dad's motorbike. As soon as the police had told dad what had happened, he slapped me right round the back of the head and I went flying across the room. Dad had never hit me before and I had never seen him so angry. He just looked at me and shouted, "Have we not been through enough? Now you bring the police to my door."

Luckily for me, the police decided to just caution me because they were happy for my dad to sort me out. The police did stress, though, that next time they would not be so lenient. "Don't worry officer, there will not be a next time', he will be in his bedroom for the year," my dad said, angrily. Well, I was in my room for the next two weeks and it may as well have been a year. By now, Tish had a boyfriend and he worked down the fish market and he said that he would try and get me some work to keep me out of trouble. Once again dad told me to get back down the gym. Once I got there, Steve just looked at me and said, "Is this another comeback?

"Steve," I said," I need to get back fighting, go back to the championships. I'm getting a job down the fish market on the Old Kent Road". Tish's boyfriend did manage to get me a start on the fish market, that was a wakeup call in more ways than one I can tell you. My hours were 4am until 2pm, six days a week. Because of the unsociable hours, I never had a chance to meet up with my friends. After three months I started gutting fish. The early starts were tough but I was getting into a routine now. I was back in the gym, getting good money, and was approaching my 16th birthday. Saturday night was my only night off. Sometimes I would go to the pub with Harry. I was still very small for my age so if we went to a club the older boys had shoved me through the window at the back. Harry was taller and had a moody ID. It was funny because the bouncers always looked at me at the end of the night and said to each other, 'How did that little fucker get in'.

Even at work I would get stick because of my size and get thrown into the Lobster tanks and get dragged around the wet floors. I even used to hide in the bellies of the Tunas after they had been gutted so no one could find me. Les and Jackie, who owned the South Bank Fresh Fish Company, said I was lucky that I was small and I made them laugh otherwise getting pulled around the floor would have been the least of my worries. As long as the work was done Les and Jackie turned a blind eye to my shenanigans. Les was well into his sport and loved Cricket and Rugby but his greatest love was Football. He was a massive QPR fan so you can imagine the banter we had with me being a member of the Millwall faithful. Les always supported my boxing as

67

well. Jackie was a small petit, no nonsense blonde lady. The company had about 30 employees, mainly men but believe me, when she got the hump, everyone stood still and took notice. She scared the bloody life out of me when she was in that mood. Saying that, Jackie was very kind and if you worked hard, she would look after you. Especially on Saturday. If I was going to Millwall, she would say, "you off to the Den today, Pete?" And if I said, 'yes' she would ask me to come into the office before I leave and bunged me a few quid. But before she handed over the money she would always say, "but no drinking". Les, with a smile and a wink would always follow on by saying, "just Guinness or two but behave yourself and see on Monday".

Chapter 15
Tish drops a bombshell.

Christmas was always a difficult time for my dad, and as the festive holidays, and my birthday, drew nearer so dad began to struggle more and more. Not only was he missing my mum but he had all us kids to worry about as well. And he was still working seven days a week to keep a roof over our heads, and feed and clothe us. Understandably, dad needed a release and maybe his way of dealing with all the pressure was to take himself off to his room with a bottle of Whiskey and his wedding album and cry himself to sleep.

I would be lying if I said it did not get to me but Martin was only 10 years old and us older kids had to be strong for him and try and function as normally as possible. Anyway, this Christmas(1992) was going to be different because I was working and I had money in my pocket so everyone got some nice presents for once. In the past I would go into Tish's room around September time, borrow some of her make up and perfume and wrap it up in Christmas paper. On Christmas Eve I would put her presents under the tree and pass them off as new. I say Christmas tree but all it was really was a house plant with bit of Tinsel around it. The next day Tish would open her presents and always looked surprised, which made me and Martin smile even more. Of course, she knew I was the cheeky sod that 'borrowed' her make up but it was all part of the fun. By this time Liam had moved out to live with his girlfriend, Jean. She had two small children but he would always invite us round to pick up our presents.

For obvious reasons the fish trade was really busy around Christmas time. And I was working 15 hour days to help keep up with all the big Hotel and Restaurant orders. All I was doing was working and sleeping. I remember getting home after yet another long day and Tish was there waiting. She said she had something to tell me but we had to wait for everyone to get home. Once Dad and Martin were home and Liam had called over around 7pm, Tish broke her news. I'll never forget it. It was one of those horrible cold evenings where the wind and rain was crashing against the windows. All of a sudden Tish just burst out crying and announced that she was pregnant. No sooner had the words come out of her mouth, me and Martin turned and looked at each other before seeing what dad's reaction would be. Liam immediately congratulated her and gave her cuddle. Tish had always been a mum to me and Martin, anyway, so it really was not that different other than she was going to have her own child. It was the first time that my dad had ever shown real emotion, though. After we had all had time to take in what Tish had said she gave us all a big cuddle and said, "Look, I'm still here for you, anything you need or if you want to talk. And of course, I'm still going to collect Martin from school".

I was happy for Tish but looking back on it I took the news quite hard. I started taking days off work, missing the gym, spending more time in the pub and hanging out with the wrong people. There were not many rules in Bermondsey but we had our morals. Not sure why I suddenly went into self-destruct mode after hearing Tish announce her pregnancy but it was about to get a whole lot worse.

To this day, I cannot for the life of me understand why I bought a motorbike. Anyone that knows me will tell you that I'm pretty unpredictable at the best of times but this was extreme, even for me. I had never driven a motorbike before and I never even had a licence or insurance. Oh, and did I mention it was a bloody super bike as well! I just thought how hard could it be? I had seen many a boy racer whizzing up and down the Old Kent Road and often thought, 'I'll have some of that'. Anyway, it was now the height of summer and there I was dressed in shorts and a t-shirt and the proud owner of a superbike, and now was as good a time as any to give it a test drive. I started her up, had a little drive around the estate and suddenly I was ready for the open road. Before I knew it, I was practically flying up and down the

Jamaica Road in Bermondsey at nearly 100mph like a seasoned veteran when suddenly, the lights turned red. As I hit the breaks the bike slid on the front wheel and as the oncoming traffic fast approached my life literally flashed before me and I could see all my childhood memories, all my family one by one hovering in front of me. All of a sudden, I came to an abrupt stop. I can remember thinking, I'm not dead. There was blood everywhere and the bike was a good 50 metres away. All the cars around me were at a standstill thinking I must be dead. I was still in that much of a shock I didn't know what was going on. As soon as I knew where I was and gathered my thoughts I got up. I was in that much of a panic thinking the police were going to turn up and nick me for having no licence and insurance that I managed to somehow get the bike out of the road and push it into some sheds away from the road and hide it. As I came out of the shed an older man shouts out, 'Are you ok son?' As I looked up it was my dad's friend Mick the Dog. My dad had a name for everyone. Mick was always with his pet Jack Russell, rain, wind or shine so everyone knew him as Mick the Dog. Mick took me to the pub but after a while I started to feel the pain and was bleeding pretty heavily so he took back to his place and patched me up. Mick said there was police everywhere. "I saw everything", said Mick. "I honestly thought you was dead". I told Mick my life flashed before me and he said, "when you got up, looked around and pushed the bike out of the road I thought it was a miracle". By now the pain was getting much worse and Mick insisted I needed to go to hospital. But I explained I couldn't because I had no licence or insurance and would get nicked if I went and got patched up. I asked him for some pain killers so he gave me half a bottle of Whiskey. That seemed to do the trick and I soon fell asleep. When I woke up, I begged Mick not to tell my dad. He said, "don't worry, I won't tell your dad, I'm just glad you're ok".

It took me a good few weeks for the body to heal and to get back to something like normal. I still to this day cannot work out how I walked away from that crash but it was a real lesson learned and I have not been on a motorbike since.

Chapter 16

Tish becomes a mum and I fight my best mate.

When I woke up in the morning Tish was always there for us to make breakfast and generally set us up for the day. But this particular day she was nowhere to be seen. I ran down to dad and asked him where she was. "she's gone to hospital with her boyfriend, she's having the baby," said dad. "I'm not going to work today, dad," I said. I quickly got dressed and jumped on the first bus to St Thomas' Hospital. I waited outside that hospital ward for what seemed like hours and quizzed every single doctor and nurse that walked past. I had been there since 3am and every now and again the scream of new born baby would bellow from between one delivery room or another. But there was still no news on Tish's new arrival. I was looking out of the window, it had just stopped raining and just as I saw a beautiful magical rainbow appear Tish's boyfriend came running out of the ward with a big smile on his face to say, "Pete, you're an uncle, it's a boy. He's like a boxer, his hands are up. He's gonna be a boxer just like you". It was April 1,1992. I rushed to see Tish and my new born nephew. I ran in to give Tish a cuddle and as soon as I looked at the baby, I fell in love with him straightaway. All them feelings I had about 'what about us' just disappeared. She had practically brought me and Martin up. As I said earlier, she was like a mum. But now, it was time for me to grow up. I was an uncle now, time to step up." 'What you gonna call him", I said, excitedly. 'Harry', came the prompt reply. "Like Harry, my best mate Harry? I said. "Yes, like your best mate Harry," she replied. There was only one way to celebrate as far as I was concerned and that was to ring Harry and tell him the good news, so that's what I did. "Harry I'm gonna be an uncle and guess what, Tish has named the baby, Harry, after you so let's get out and wet the baby's head". I was so happy but I think I was drinking too much, even on weekdays. I was not really doing anything with my life and only playing at boxing.

Not long after my nephew was born, I started training for the ABA's but as I said I was not living the life of a dedicated sportsman so that meant me entering a weight division above the light welterweight category I was comfortable with. I did ok in the first south east semi-final beating Adam Martin from Fitzroy Lodge which meant I had to face my Fisher clubmate Leo O'Reilly in the final. It was a decent scrap but Leo beat me on points and once again I went on the missing list.

To be fair to my coach Steve (Hiser), kept ringing me asking what I was doing. I did say I'd be back soon, and I was back but instead of training six days a week like I did before I was only going to the gym twice. By the time the ABA championships came around a year later I was back in the gym and even heavier than before. The No.1 welterweight at the Fisher at the time was my best friend growing up, Elvis Mbwakongo. I was Irish and Elvis was black. And although Steve treated us all equal and like sons, I just felt we were the odd ones out.

With my weight the way it was I half expected Steve to say, 'Pete, I'm not putting you in the ABA's unless you can make light-welter'. And that's exactly what he said. And I said, "if you don't put me in the ABA's then I'll never fight again". It was a bit naughty of me really because Steve knew I going down the wrong path and boxing was all that kept me on straight and narrow. And also, Steve was like a father figure to me because my dad was working seven days a week, 12 hours a day to put food on the table and a roof over our heads. Dad would leave for work in the dark and come home in the dark. He never liked me boxing, he said it was dangerous but he knew that it kept me out of trouble.

Eventually Steve gave in and allowed me to enter the ABA's at welterweight instead of a division below, where I should have been if I was more disciplined. The only problem me fighting at welterweight was that I would have to fight my best mate, Elvis. We had grown up together and had a close bond. Elvis was from the Congo and we had experienced bullying and racism together so the last thing you want to do is fight your best mate in front of a crowd of people. The good thing about Amateur and pro boxing is everyone is equal. Racism, colour, whatever issue it was all left at the gym door, so it was a great escape from everyday life.

The day finally came when Elvis and me came together to face each other in the ring at the Crystal Palace National Sports Centre in South London. As I said, Steve never took sides so we both had neutral coaches. We were not even allowed to have any friends or family there to support us. Funny thing was we were allowed to get ready in the same changing room and even warmed up to the same music. We even walked to the ring together. It was a crazy night because the place should have been buzzing but you could hear a pin drop. I think the boxers from the other clubs had told their fans we were best mates from the same club. Even when our names were called there was a respectful clap in appreciation of what was to come. There was definitely a 1,000 plus people in the hall but I swear only five people were clapping.

Once the bell rang our friendship went out of the window as we tried to take each other's head off. It really was a real barnstormer, both of us gave it our all. Once the fight was over, we both looked into each other's eyes and with tears streaming down our faces, we both said, 'we are glad that's over'. As the judges collected up their scorecards the ring announcer said, "Never saw this fight happening but this is what amateur boxing is all about. Put your hands together for two great friends and warriors". The whole place went crazy as Elvis won a split decision. As I gave Elvis a cuddle I said," you deserved it I never should have entered at welterweight". For some reason Elvis always used to call me McDonagh. Maybe he could not remember my first name but I expect it was because our trainer Steve Hiser always called me McDonagh as well. Back in the changing room afterwards Elvis gave me a bit of a lecture, only a good friend would be able to get away with. "Take this boxing serious McDonagh, you will be a champion. Train with me for next year's championships, you can do lightweight. Win some club shows and stay out of the pub you piss head. Do you want to a champion and make your family proud? "Of course I do," I
74

said. "Your friend Harry is a good man but the other friends you got are no good for you". I knew Elvis was right and I did agreed to train with him. So, the very next morning at 6am we went for a run around Southwark Park Hills.

Shortly after agreeing to knuckle down and train properly I spoke to Jackie and Les about cutting my hours down so I could train properly. I never needed much money. Afterall, all I was doing was training, sleeping and eating. I soon started seeing the hard work pay off in the gym and running up the hills. The weight started dropping off and every fight I had felt better than before. I think I had 16 fights leading up to the ABA's and only lost one. I was flying. Before my new found enthusiasm I was a win two lose in three type of fighter. I was practically living in the gym at this time, six days a week. I was ranked No.5 at light welter in the British rankings but no one knew I was going to enter the ABA's a division below at lightweight.

Getting punched in the face day in day was hard but I was determined to keep my promise to Elvis and make my family proud of me. The word soon got around that I was entering the ABA's at lightweight. There were quite a few people that thought I could go all the way but equally, there were those that thought I had more chance of finding Lord Lucan riding Shergar than me making 60kgs.

The important thing, though, was Steve started believing in me. He proved that by putting a lot more time into me and I really started to improve, both as a boxer and a person. For the first time I had the right attitude. This was also the first time I really found out just how powerful the mind could be because I was determined to train my mind to get down to lightweight, which meant sticking to a strict training regime and the right nutritional diet. It was not long before my new found improved attitude and discipline was to be tested as Christmas was fast approaching and it took all my will powers of resilience to swerve the Christmas puddings and pints of Guinness. But I was focused and still determined to stick to the plan.

It was also a sad time because Tish was having a hard time with her little boy Harry's father. He was not very nice to her so she decided to move back to Ireland with Harry, which obviously upset us all. Tish moving really broke dad's heart but as long as it made Tish happy that was all we cared about. We spoke to her most nights on the phone and she came back often, and Me and Martin went to see her as well so it worked out fine.

Chapter 17
Wrong place wrong time

Christmas Eve, 2000 was a date I will never forget, and not just because we were a week away from celebrating the Millennium. As I said earlier the fish trade is always busy around Christmas and New Year because all the Hotels and Restaurants increase their orders to cater for the extra business. After a long day I could not wait to get home and have a bath and wash away the stale smell of Fish. Having a bath in our house back then was a feat in itself because Martin wanted to keep pets, so me like an idiot brought home two crayfish for him. I used to have to clean the bath out every time I wanted to use it. And every time someone wanted a bath Martin would shout up, 'Make sure Ronnie and Reggie are ok'

No sooner had I got out of the bath the phone rang, it was my brother Liam. He only lived a 10 minute walk away, with his girlfriend Jean and the kids, Joey and Billy. Liam asked if I'd like to go over and see him so I said I would be there in an hour. I just wanted to get out of the house for a bit because if I'd stayed in, I would have been bored. In any case it took my mind off raiding the fridge. So, I put my tracksuit on and headed out the door and the short walk down the Jamaica Road. If you know Bermondsey then you will know that walking down the Jamaica Road can take forever because back then it was a very close community where everyone knew everyone. I was about two minutes away from Liam's when someone shouted over from the Prince of Wales pub, which was my local. It was a friend of mine called

Jonathan. Me and Jonathan had been altar boys together at the Church and went to school together but I had not seen him for years. Johnathon said, "I have not seen you in ages". I told him I have been training for the ABA's so not been out much. After a brief chat, Jonathon said, "it's been ages since I've seen you, pop in for half a Guinness so we can have a chat". I did not know it at the time but saying yes to having half a pint of Guinness was soon going to be a decision I would live to regret.

When I got in the pub Jonathon was with a few other people I knew but they were not friends of mine or locals at the Prince of Wales. I did know other people in there and before I knew it everyone was buying me drinks and wishing me Merry Christmas. So much for half a pint of Guinness! Anyone that knows a boxer will tell you that once we start, we can't stop. I just thought, 'It's Christmas, one day off won't hurt and I'll go for a run tomorrow'. I also convinced myself that after training so hard I had justified coming off the wagon, albeit briefly. Then Jonathon suggested we take a walk down the Blue Anchor, about 20 a minute walk away. Good thing about Bermondsey is everything is a short walk away, either through alleyways or estates. There was about six of us but Jonathon was the only one I could call a friend. Once we got in the Blue Anchor I was on my way and the Guinness was flowing, and I was in the Christmas spirit. By the time we moved on to the Foresters Arms across the road I had forgotten all about going to Liam's house. The Foresters was a proper Millwall pub. The fans went there before all the home games. Jonathan was a massive Millwall fan but a very quiet good natured man that would not hurt a fly. We had a few pints in the Foresters. The pub was absolutely rammed.. Then a few people started fighting and someone got a pool que smashed over their head. It involved a few people around our company so we all got kicked out. By now I have had enough and said I'm off home. But a few of the boys said, 'Come on its Christmas Eve let's have a few more pints in the Blue Anchor?' Like I said earlier, I had had a few pints of the black stuff and did not need persuading too much when it came to a few more. When we got back to the Blue Anchor there was a funny vibe in there. There was about five people in there and four of us. After talking to Jonathon for a while he decided to call it a night and a make his way home. I said I would walk back with the other two. "One more drink Barman," I shouted over. 'You have had enough,' he replied. So, we finished our game of pool and made for the exit. After sinking a good few pints, we were in good spirits as we walked up Blue Anchor Lane. Unfortunately, there was one person we encountered that night that was not in a very festive mood. It was one of those dark, windy and cold nights and there were very few street lamps on. As we walked slowly up the road without a care in the world one of the boys I was with shouted 'Merry Christmas' to a man across the road. The man quickly looked over and said, 'Who the fucking hell do you think you're talking to'. That was it then because the same lad replied, 'Fuck you then'. With that the man ran across the road shouting and muttering something. I couldn't for the life of me understand what he was saying but that was the least of my worries because a split second later, as he got nearer, I could first see a gleam of light in his right hand and then as he got even closer, I could see it was definitely a dirty great knife. The whole thing was like slow motion and I just thought, 'this is it, I'm a dead man'. Then, as quick as a flash one of the lads I was with came up from the side and cracked the fella on the jaw and he went down like a sack of potatoes. As the fella lay motionless on the deck the second kid I was with, ran up and kicked him in the head a few times. At the time I didn't think nothing of it because he was just knocked out and a little of blood coming out of his nose. So, we just left him and carried on walking home. And he did have a knife in his hand and I'm pretty sure he was going to stab me.

When I got home Tish said, 'Your late, Liam rang and said you didn't turn up at his house, and you've been drinking, where have you been?' I just said I had had a couple of pints with some mates. The truth of the matter was I had had a right skinful of the black stuff but had sobered up pretty quickly after nearly getting stabbed again. Looking death in the face can have that effect on a person.

Tish asked if I was ok, I said I was fine but tired so was going to bed. I woke up about 9am Christmas morning, just in time to watch Tish and my nephew, Harry open their presents which was a nice distraction from having to remember the events of the night before. I had bought Harry a Millwall kit. He loved it and always wore it when I took him to the home games when he was over from Ireland. It was a great day. I was a bit worse for wear but nothing like a good slow run to sweat out the Guinness, followed by a fry up, could not sort out.

We were all in good spirits and my dad was happy enough sitting there with a cigarette in one hand and a hot Whisky with sugar in the other. He was pretty quiet for quite a while as if he was thinking about something. Then all of a sudden, in his thick Irish accent, he asked, 'What time did you get in last night, Peter? "Not too late," I said. Quick as a flash, he replied, 'It was about one o'clock. Was you drinking? I said I had had a couple but he knew I drank a skinful. 'What you doing drinking, I thought you were boxing soon?

"I am boxing soon," but just as I was going to make up some excuse no one would ever believe he turned his attention to the ITV news on the television. Tish told him to turn the tv off because she wanted to question me some more but dad always watched the news. He loved finding out was going on in the world. I wish he bloody hadn't because the newsreader announced there was, 'News just in that a man had been brutally attacked and was fighting for his life in hospital'. The bulletin went on to say that the attack happened around 11pm on Blue Anchor Lane in Bermondsey and the police were appealing for witnesses.

News travelled fast in Bermondsey back in the 90's. The internet was very much in its infancy but the local grapevine was more than a match for any of today's social media platforms. Tish looked straight over to me and asked if I had heard anything but just said, 'no, not a thing'. I just sat there but the shock of what happened just kept going around in my mind. Even though I'd had a good few pints of Guinness I decided the only thing that was going to clear my head was to go for a run. I had visions of going on the run because even though only three of us actually knew exactly what happened I thought it was only a matter of time before I got a knock at the door. While I was out running, people kept stopping to say, 'Pete, have you heard about what happened on Blue Anchor Lane last night, it's all over the news? Of course, I just said I had not heard a thing. Like I said news travels fast and there were all sorts of rumours flying about.

Once I got home, I just sat in the bath and thought to myself, 'I'm fucked'. It was Christmas Day and there was a big dinner on the table but I just could not face it. I was starving but my stomach was churning

79

around inside as the realisation of what happened the night before kicked in. Everyone was pulling crackers and laughing but I just made an excuse that my weight was a bit on the heavy side and needed to miss a meal or two. As the days went by, I was getting more and more anxious. I couldn't help wondering if the man was going to die or whether the police were going to knock on the front door at any moment. It also did not help that every time News At 10 was broadcast they mentioned the assault and were still appealing for witnesses.

A week or so later I went back to the Fisher to train for the ABA's and also to take my mind off everything. I was not even staying at home in case the police came knocking. Instead, I got my head down at Liam's and Jean's flat about, 10 minutes away. Dad and Tish did ask why I was stopping at Liam's, I made the excuse that Jean cooked healthier meals which was better for me to keep my weight down. After the gym one night my coach Steve said he would drop me home. If we were in the gym late, he would always drop me off. I explained to Steve that I was staying at Liam's and he asked me, why? I told him the same as I told my dad and Tish, the food was healthier and it helped in keeping my weight down. Steve did admit that my weight was looking good and that if I continued to progress, I had a real chance of winning the ABA title this year. I honestly thought Steve had bought my story but he was far from daft. He knew all us young boxers inside out, better than we knew ourselves. That's why he was such a good coach because he knew us all individually, what made us tick and how to get the best out of us. He also knew when we were trying to get one over on him as well. So, I was not surprised when he said, "are you sure everything is ok? And have you heard anything about the attack on Blue Anchor Lane?

I could not very well say I had not heard about it because everyone from lands' End to John O'Groats had heard about it. Afterall, it was on the bloody national news, so I could not avoid it. "It never had anything to do with you, did it? replied Steve. "No of course not", I said. As I got out of the car I remember thinking, 'He bloody knows it was something to do with me but couldn't prove it'.

It was now January 5, about two weeks after the attack. As I was relaxing around Liam's the news came on and it was announced that two men had been arrested for the attempted murder in Blue Anchor Lane, Bermondsey on Christmas Eve. Apparently, clothing had been found in a bush with my DNA on it. Less than 24 hours later the moment I had been dreading every day since the attack happened, suddenly became a reality. As my dad was sitting at home minding his own business the murder squad kicked in the front door looking for me. As they turned the house upside down, one of the officers picked up a picture of me on the sideboard and said, 'Where's your son? My dad said he had no clue but as soon as they left, he phoned Liam and told him the police had been there looking for me. Dad said, "who has he murdered? It must be serious because they were plain clothed and had guns".

Liam tried to reassure dad that it must be a mistake and they must have mixed him up with someone else but dad said that they had left a contact number and I was to ring them straight away. When I got back from the Fisher Club. Liam ordered me to sit down. He was really angry and in no uncertain terms he shouted, "did you have anything to do with that attempted murder on Blue Anchor Lane at Christmas? I said, "no, why? "Because the murder squad have just kicked in dad's front door and ripped the place apart, that why," Liam shouted back.

I just could not carry on lying the way I was to everyone that asked. I was tired of keeping it to myself and the burden of guilt at being there was really started to drain me physically and mentally. It was time to come clean. "I was there but I never did anything," which was true. Still shouting at the top of his voice, Liam said, "you had better sort it because they are looking for you and I don't want them kicking my door in and turning the place upside down with the kids here". Of course, he was right. I would not have the kids go through that, either.

Once he had let off some steam Liam told me to stay where I was and he was going to go out and speak to someone. An hour or so later Liam came back and said that he had made an appointment for me to see a local solicitor by the name of Paul Robinson. Paul was the solicitor quite a few local people used and he advised me to hand myself in to the police right away, but not until he had a chance to get me one of his solicitors to go with me. Paul said just keep your head down until I call you.

I decided to ring Elvis and tell him to pick me up from the solicitor's office. I told him I needed to be a way from the local area for a short time. Elvis said, "Don't worry McDonagh, I know where to go. Elvis picked me up and we drove along the Old Kent Road and parked up at the local McDonalds. If you do not know the Old Kent Road, it is one of the busiest roads in London. As we pulled in Elvis said, "don't worry McDonagh, no one will find you here". Was he fucking serious? I must have bumped into about 500 people I knew. I may just as well of sat on the steps of the police station and waited for them to pick me up. Anyway, after two hours of the most nerve-wracking moment of my life I got call from the solicitor informing me to hand myself in at Walworth Police station. It was about 10 minutes away in the car and have to say it was the longest 10 minutes of my life. Elvis dropped me off. I walked in and said my name is Peter McDonagh and I have walked in on my own free will. As soon as I said that a couple of plain clothes officers rushed out and slapped the handcuffs on me. One of the officers read me my rights and said 'You are under arrest for attempted murder, you have the right to remain silent, anything which you do say can be used in evidence against you'. This was it, the point of no return.

Chapter 18
Remanded in custody.

I did argue that there was no need to handcuff me as I had entered the Police station of my own free will but that cut no ice with the old bill. As the custody sergeant booked me in and I was strip searched the realization of the trouble I was in started to set in pretty quickly. Shortly after I was processed and searched, I was put in a cell for a few hours. I think they do this sometimes to allow you to over think what's about to come and mess with your mind. It bloody worked as well because the cell stank of piss. It reminded me of the first day I arrived in Bermondsey from Ireland when I got in the lift at Giles House on the Dickens Estate. From there the unhappy memories came flooding back to me. My mum being drunk all the time, her hitting my sister and brother, and abusing my dad. These were serious flashbacks for me. I can honestly say I was not worried about the police. I was more worried about how my dad was going to react when I got out. After the incident with the motor cycle and everything dad had been through, the only thing he asked from us kids was to, 'never bring the police my door'. I felt I let him down and when that cell door slammed shut my mind was racing faster than a Formula One car around a race track. My old breadbox was well and truly scrambled now and I was certainly not thinking straight, so my theory that the police leave you to stew in the cells to mess up your thought processes was well founded in my opinion. I was offered food and drink but I refused, all I wanted was my one phone call I was entitled to, and I banged on that cell door until I got it. Eventually, I got my wish and called Liam. I told him to tell dad

I'm ok and that I had done nothing wrong. The other person I told him to ring was Steve Hiser, my boxing coach and tell him the same thing.

Once I had finished my one phone call I was taken back to the cells and left for a good couple of hours until the Custody Sergeant banged on the door again informing me that it was time to be interviewed. Even though I was left for good few hours on my own I could not get my head down, so I was pretty tired by the time I was walking to the interview room. Just before I got there a small man appeared in front of me. "Hello Mr McDonagh, my name's John and I'm your solicitor, and I have been asked to represent you by Paul Robinson's office". The first thing John did was to inform the CID officers that he wanted a brief word with me in private before any official interview began so we went into an office with no cameras or microphones.

As soon as we were alone the first thing John said to me was, "I want you to be open and honest with me, Mr McDonagh. This is an attempted murder investigation. The man is in intensive care and this could easily turn into a murder investigation." I will never forget those words as long as I live. I felt the blood drain from my face and remember thinking, 'this is serious'.

I just told the truth, I said, "I was there but I never done nothing and never saw anything" The solicitor said, 'ok, you will be asked lots of questions in different ways and they will try and get you to talk, but my advice to you is to give a no comment interview'. So that's what I did, said 'no comment' to every single question. I was in there for what seemed like an eternity. It was the first time I had experienced anything like that before and I felt like they were trying to break me down. They just kept repeating the same thing over and over again. I remember thinking, 'I can understand now why some people admit to things, even when they are innocent'.

Thankfully, John the brief was there to guide me and when he thought I was getting tired or vulnerable he requested a break. As we left the room, the tape was turned off and John turned to me and said, 'you're doing fine Mr McDonagh, I still advise you to no comment'. A short while after the interview restarted the CID officer in charge decided he had heard enough and that he was going to bail me. For anyone that is not familiar with the bail process it means that the police are still gathering evidence but I could go home. It also meant that I had to report to the Police Station every day at 4pm with my passport. The investigation was far from over, in fact, it had only just begun, but I more worried about what my dad and my coach, Steve had to say. Liam's wife Jean and her cousin James came and picked me up, then dropped me back home.

As soon as I got through the front door, I could see dad sitting in his armchair with his usual glass of Whiskey in one hand and a cigarette in the other. All he said very sternly to me was, "you have just been on the news. Well, they didn't mention your name but the police said four people have been bailed pending further investigation". He then turned away in disgust. I said I was so tired after being questioned for half the night all I wanted to do was go to bed. Sarcastically, dad replied, "you better get used to it, you could be in there for a long time". No sooner had I said, I had not done anything wrong, dad shouted," well what the fuck have they arrested you for then?

If the last few days were not stressful enough for me, it was about to get a whole lot worse when I went back down the Fisher to face my coach, Steve and the rest of the boys. When I walked through the door it felt like the very first time, I have ever walked in there all those years ago. As soon as Steve and the other boxers set eyes on me everything stopped. You could have heard a pin drop, it was that eerily silent until, Steve let rip from the other side of the gym, "McDonagh, what the fucks going on, you told me you never knew anything about that fight in Blue Anchor Lane? What did I say about using boxing outside the gym? Come outside I want to speak to you"

I had never seen Steve like this before, he was proper giving me the hair dryer treatment. "Why did you lie to me McDonagh? "Steve, I promise I was there, but I never threw a punch". Steve looked me straight in the eyes and shouted," If I find out you're lying to me McDonagh you will never set foot in this gym again. Now get in that gym, I want to check your weight, the ABA's are in 10 days' time". Luckily for me I was only pound over the lightweight limit, which was like a bloody miracle since I had drunk half the profits of the Guinness factory on Christmas eve. The main thing was, Steve was happy with my weight after training that night, and that pound soon disappeared. I just wanted to train hard so I could forget about the serious trouble I was in. As always, my old mate Elvis was as positive as ever, saying "Don't worry McDonagh, you will be fine". That was easy for him to say but four days later I got a call from Paul, the solicitor, saying that I had to report to the police station to appear in an identification parade. One of Paul's solicitors, John was there and briefed me about what to do. He said, "you will be in a line-up of 10 people, who will all look similar to you in height, looks and size, you won't see these people until you go in the room. They are like actors; they do this for a living. They will also ask you where you want to stand between one and 10.

John told me that there were four witnesses there that night that saw what went on so you will have to stand in four different line ups. They will not see or talk to each other. They will come in at all different times. I went in the room and when I saw the other nine, they were completely different to me in both height and looks. I remember thinking, 'are they setting me up? I also thought, 'It is what its is', I can't change anything so have to just get on with it.

When I lined up, I had to face the front. There was a dark screen directly in front to protect the identity of the witness but if you focus hard enough you can a shadow walking up and down the line. I saw them stopping and staring. Then the policeman in charge told us all to turn to our sides. I could see the shadows on the other side of the glass moving in nearer the screen to get a better look. I wasn't sure whether the first three witnesses picked me out, but I had a feeling the fourth one did. Once the identity parade was over, myself and my other co-defendants were taken to another room, where the officer in charge announced that we were all going to be taken from Camberwell Police station to Orpington Police station.

I can remember thinking, 'that's miles away. We were all taken in separate cars and accompanied by four CID officers. Can you imagine doing that nowadays, especially with the price of petrol! I was squashed between two officers and hand cuffed to each one. By this time, I was starving and one of the officers suggested we stopped at a McDonalds on the way. One asked if I wanted anything but I just said, 'No comment'. Which was a bloody stupid thing to say because the burgers smelt great and I was bloody hungry. When we arrived at Orpington the place was empty in terms of prisoners so the four of us had the place to ourselves. We were all put in separate cells but we all left flaps open so we could talk. Talking about the I D parade one of the lads said 'do you think you was picked out Pete? You didn't even do anything. This bloke just came across the road with a knife, what does anyone expect us to do, just stand and let him stab us?

After they let us stew in the cells for what seemed like an eternity, the officer in charge started pulling us all in for interview, one by one. I refused to go anywhere until I got my phone call. After about 12 hours I was eventually let out to have my phone call. I called my brother, Liam, told him where I was and to bring us all up McDonalds. Liam said, do not discuss anything about the case because them cells are bugged. When I got back to the cells, I told the boys not to say a thing because the place was bugged. But they all just started laughing before loudly breaking out into a song called Buggin, the one sung by Dane Bowers.

By now it was coming up to the time to either charge us or let us go. I'll never forget it because one by one they took us all out of our cells to announce that we were all going to get charged with attempted murder. Once we were all back in the cells the tone of our behaviour changed dramatically as the reality of the situation finally sunk that we were in serious trouble. We were told that we will be going to court in the morning, but first we were taken to have our finger prints, photos and forensic swabs taken, before yet another round in of interview interrogation.

During my interview I was shown pictures of what the man looked like after the attack and told he was in intensive care at St Thomas Hospital. It was a worrying time and to keep my mind active I did a bit of training in my cell in case, by some miracle I was suddenly released and could enter the ABA's. I did some shadow boxing, press ups and sit ups. At about 7am in the morning the cell door opened and the custody officer came in and informed me that, 'it was time for court'. Before I knew it two man mountain security guards had handcuffed me, one to each of my wrists, and more or less picked me up and threw me into a prison van. Regular users of this mode of transport to and from prison refer to these as sweat boxes. They are made up of a number of very small little boxes, five down one side and five down the other with just enough room for a seat and a small window to look out of. No one can see in and when the sun is beaming through, it really does get tropical in there and very claustrophobic.

Because we had a police escort in front of us it did not take us long to travel from Orpington to Tower Bridge Magistrates court. As soon as we arrived at court I looked out of the small window and saw my brothers Martin and Liam, and my dad, Bill waiting on the corner. I banged on the window like a madman to try and get their attention but of course it was no use. Funny thing was my dad was waving but I expect he was waving to every bloody van that arrived at court that morning.

If you have ever wondered what happens when these vans arrive at court, I'll tell you. The van drives into a fenced off area and once secured the guard open's the sweatbox door but leaves it on a chain while they handcuff you through the gap. Then they march you off to the holding cells, that are located under the court room allocated to you. Before you are summoned up the steps to face the judge you are visited by your solicitor to be briefed on what will happen. As this was a preliminary hearing, the only thing to discuss was whether or not I would be granted bail or be remanded in custody. I'd never been to court before so this was all new to me. I explained to my solicitor that I needed to get bail because I was due to box in the ABA's in 10 days' time. Shows how much I knew about how these things work because I honestly thought I would not have a problem getting bail, but my brief soon put paid to that by telling me in no uncertain terms that there was, 'No chance you are getting bail today'. He basically said, 'this is a big case and it looks like you will be remanded so get yourself prepared and ready to go to prison'. So, myself and my three co-defendants were marched up the steps to be put in front of the judge. As our families supported us from the public gallery, the judge read out the charges against us. He also said that the attempted murder charges against us were far too serious to be heard in a magistrate's court so we would be remanded in custody to appear at the Old Bailey in seven days. 'Take them down,' announced the judge. I looked across to the public gallery and saw my dad with his head in his hands. When he looked up, he had tears in his eyes. I was sad inside, not just for me but also for my family but I put on a brave smile and told dad I'll be ok.

Two of the defendants were only 19 so they were shipped off to a young offender's prison while myself and the fourth defendant were whisked off to HMP Brixton. As we got loaded back into the sweatbox for the short trip to Brixton my emotions were all over the place. I'd never been to prison before and I'd be lying if I said I was not a little worried about what I was walking into. It is bad enough knowing you are going to spend time at Her Majesty's pleasure but when you drive through those big gates and they slam shut behind you, the reality of how much trouble I was in left me in no doubt. Brixton was the oldest prison in London. It was built in 1820 and believe me, it had not been updated much since then. Back in the 90's it still had a reputation for extreme violence and severe overcrowding.

As I walked in to experience prison life for the first time the screw met me at the door and said, 'Is this your first time in prison, son? He did not really have to ask, my face told him all he needed to know. 'From now on McDonagh you will be known by your prison number, GF 568LM'.

Chapter 19
Prisoner GF 568LM

The one thing you must do when you are in prison is never ever show any weakness because if you do every low life scumbag will jump all over you and take a liberty. I knew as soon as I got there, I had put on this exterior bravado even though inside I was shitting myself. Anyone that says they are not scared when they go to prison for the first time is either a liar or has a few brain cells missing. But the one thing I was not prepared for was being totally stripped, quite literally, of my dignity in three seconds flat.

After booking in at the 'Brixton Hilton' a screw appeared from nowhere and ordered us new intakes to stand in line and take off all our clothes ready for a strip search. 'You have never been in prison before have you McDonagh? said the screw. I can only assume that as I was the only one not bent over parting my arse cheeks over a mirror, that was how he knew I was new blood. I soon found out very quickly what some people would do to smuggle things into prison. Once that unpleasantry was over with we were told to get dressed before we were all put in a holding cell with all the other prisoners.

In some ways that was just as uncomfortable because, although I was in fighting shape, I was only small. Just as everyone was sizing each other up and asking what they were in for. My name got called and I was taken into an adjoining room, where a doctor in a white coat asked me lots of questions. Nowadays they would call it duty of care or some other kind of box ticking exercise. I was asked things like, 'was I thinking of self-harming? was I suicidal? I'm thinking, 'why are you asking me all these questions? The good thing was, after a few minutes the doctor said he was happy I was ok and moved me on to a wing.

If I was not shitting myself enough when we drove through those big double gates and then having some old screw invading my private space with a mirror, the next phase of my induction into prison life, definitely did.

This was it, no more messing around with questions and duty of care I was given a 'welcome pack' which consisted of a tooth brush, toiletries, knife and fork and a plate. They did ask if I wanted tobacco but I told them I didn't smoke, which was a bit silly of me because I could have swapped it for something else. Still, you live and learn, and that was something I had to do very quickly. I was soon moved on again, this time to another room, much bigger than before. They call it a holding cell, which means they put all us new inmates into whilst they decide where to put us, on what wing and with whom.

I looked around the room and saw people were going crazy, screaming, shouting and shivering in the corners. I said to one well-dressed man sitting next to me, "what's up with them? He replied," this must be your first time mate, they are all heroin addicts, on the brown stuff, they are going cold Turkey, its full of them in here".

Luckily, my name was called before we could get too deeply involved in conversation. They were calling people up two and three at a time but when they called my name it was just me, which I thought was strange. The screw led me through all these different doors, keys jangling until eventually, he shouted, "here you McDonagh, you're on three's (which meant I was on landing 3). "Your Lucky McDonagh, you're in a single cell." Lucky! you gotta be kidding me, not only was I banged up for no reason but the place was like a dungeon. Like I said, Brixton was built in the 1800's and I swear the one bed, table and sink in my cell were the original fixtures and fittings. The screw slammed the door shut behind and said, if you want exercise when we shout out, switch your light on? All I could hear was people kicking doors and shouting, and thought 'fuck this, this lot will go wild when they get let out'.

91

By now it was about 3pm. It had been a long day, going to court, being marched off to prison and then having to go through all the various processes to get to this point. The cell was cold, the bed was like a concrete slab and there was no privacy at all as the screws peered in every so often. It was a bit like being on the stage where everyone could see you. But at least I was in a single cell and could gather my thoughts. After about an hour of listening to all the other inmates shouting and swearing about being allowed out for exercise. The screw shouted out to put your light on and ring your bell if you want to come out. I put my light on and a short while later the screw opened the viewing flap on my door before unlocking it and letting me out. It had only been a few hours but I was I glad to get some fresh air in the exercise yard. It was not exactly a stroll around Hyde Park, more like a school playground with a 20 foot wall with barb wire on the top, but at least the air was fresh. As it was my first time inside I kept myself to myself. But then I saw my codefendant, who I was with at the start of the night. He was the friend from school who had called over to me at the start of the night on Christmas Eve, while I was on my way to Liam's. We were altar boys together at the Church Dockyard in Bermondsey, and old school friends. I'm not going to pretend I was not scared about being banged up with some of the most dangerous people in London but at least I was a trained boxer and a bit streetwise, my codefendant was a nice, easy going and softly spoken bloke. He was struggling, so I tried to keep him as upbeat as I could. I was innocent of what I was being accused of but I was there when the assault took place, my mate was not, so he didn't know anything. If you remember he went home early but the police found him on the CCTV camera. I think they banged him up to try and break him.

Exercise ended and I just told my old school friend to keep his head down and reassured him we would be out of here within a week. I got back to my cell and I just had a bit of a meltdown for a brief moment. As I sat on my bed peering out of the half-moon shaped window, I suddenly had a vision that the screws were going to open my cell door any minute and tell me to prepare to go to my dad's funeral and pack me off in handcuffs. He had been through a lot and I had let him down. I was all over the place but I had to find something to motivate me and I suddenly thought that I had the ABA's coming up. It was tough but I said to myself, 'you know what, I may be here physically but not mentally, I need to focus'. So, I got straight out of bed and started preparing for the national championships. First, I warmed up with a bit of shadow boxing then I got down to some floor work, sit ups, press us, squat trusts and some running on the spot. The one thing I had no problem with was getting down to the weight because the food in Brixton while I was there was only one step up from edible. For breakfast the screw used to come in with some long life milk and a box of cereal. The landing did mix on occasion to play pool, table tennis or dominoes but I was not interested. As long as I could have a shower, make some phone calls and speak to my family every day I was happy. In any case I was not going to be here long, I was going to get bail and was looking forward to boxing in the championships.

There was only so much training I could do so to pass the time away I did try and read books as much as I could but I did struggle because I always found it difficult to read and write. I was one of those kids that always dreaded having to read out aloud in class because I struggled so much. It was not until years later that I was told I suffered from Dyslexia, it's a learning disability that effects someone's reading, writing and spelling ability. But as long as I could speak to my dad every day, I was happy.

Being on remand meant I was allowed a couple of visits a week. So, my brother Liam and his wife Jean visited and so did my best mate, Elvis. The same Elvis I boxed in the ABA's the year before. Elvis tried to keep my spirits up by re-minding me to stay positive and that I have the ABA's coming up soon. He did ask how my training was going. I did say it was 'going fine but I had trouble getting sparring partners'. Elvis just laughed and said I was crazy.

The day after Elvis visited, I was woken up at 6am by the prison officer opening the door. "You ready McDonagh. Get all your things together because you will not be coming back here". I took a quick look around and said, "That's a shame Gov I was just settling in". Secretly I was shitting myself and was praying I would be home and in my own bed by tonight.

Another officer comes in says, "sorry, but we have to put the cuffs on". I was marched straight out, searched and told I was off to the Old Bailey. I had seen the Bailey plenty of times on the TV and ran past it while I was doing my road work. Never in a million years though, did I think that one day I would be up in front of the beak, myself, on an attempted murder charge.

Some of the most infamous of criminals and murderers from The Kray Twins, the Yorkshire Ripper and Dennis Nilsen were sentenced there so it was no joke where I was going. It was VIP treatment all the way this time. We left Brixton at about 7.30am and it was blue lights all the way in the sweatbox. We did not stop for nothing. Normally, this sort of treatment was only levelled at the serious armed robber or murder trials. As we arrived and drove through the big gates, all of sudden all these heavily armed police officers appeared wearing baseball caps. No one was escaping that day I can tell you. 'McDonagh, your off first'. As the box opened, I saw the officer from Brixton waiting for me. I thought that's a bit strange, so I said, "gov, how come your escorting me and not the sweatbox officer? He said, 'because your security level has changed, you're now a category A prisoner'. That was not what I wanted to hear at 8am in the morning walking into the most infamous courthouse in the UK.

As soon as I set foot off the van all I saw was a sea of flashing lights from photographers looking to get the perfect picture. I just put my blazer over my head, hid behind the officer and hurried into the building. Believe me it is no joke being handcuffed to a screw that close to you and literally breathing down your neck. The worst part for me was the hanging around in a cold cell, and the news I got before I got out of the sweatbox did not help either. I was left in cells for hours until I got a legal visit from my barrister, who told me I was seeing the judge after lunch. Before we went through the case files and the application for bail, I asked him why I was being moved up to a category A prisoner. He said it was because of all the media coverage our case was getting and the bail being set at £1 million, which was arranged by Liam and his wife. I told the barrister I was boxing in the ABA's soon but he said he had done all he could for me to get bail. I felt like I was on trial by the media even before my bail hearing was even heard.

94

As I said the worst part was being left alone in a damp and cold cell whilst awaiting my fate but that was matched equally by the disgusting food, they had the cheek to pass off as sausage and mash. Believe me, if my coach Steve had any reservations about me making weight for the ABA's he need not have worried. Once lunch was over the cell door opened and the screw shouted, 'McDonagh, you're in court one'. As I walked up those famous steps into court one, it actually felt quite eerie because the stairs were really creaky and I was also getting chills go through me thinking the bloody Yorkshire Ripper or Dennis Nilsen may well have climbed the same steps.

As I walked into the dock my three codefendants were already there. I looked up to the public gallery and saw my dad, Liam, his wife Jean and my little brother Martin. Although, quietly shitting myself, I did put on a brave face, smiled and gave my family the thumbs up before sitting down. Moments later we were all told to rise before the Judge entered the court. I will never forget that judge as he looked straight at me. He was an angry looking man of about 70 years old, with those old-fashioned half-moon glasses they used to wear back then.

Bail hearings are very short. A judge will either grant bail or explain why bail is denied and the defendant should be remanded in custody. This court appearance was no different. The Judge read out the charges and the prosecution read out their statement which, as you can imagine, did not help our cause to be bailed one little bit. As soon as the prosecutor said, "they are all a danger to the public and this was a horrific attack", I thought to myself, 'there will be no ABA's for you Peter, not a chance of bail'. Even though my Barrister pleaded my case and insisted bail conditions were in place for me the judge very sternly announced that, "I remand Peter McDonagh to Belmarsh High Security Prison until the next court date".

Chapter 20
Next stop Belmarsh high security prison

Hearing that judge remand me to custody really shook me up, but looking up at my family in the public gallery and seeing the tears run down my dad's face was as upsetting and as painful as anything I had experienced in my life up until then. But again, I knew I had to be brave, I had to be positive for dad's sake. As they took me back down the creaky staircase, I shouted to dad that I would keep training hard and be back home soon.

Before I knew it I was back in the Prison van (Sweatbox) and whisked away to my new home, HMP Belmarsh in south London. For some reason the trip to Belmarsh took us south of the river through my neck of the woods in Bermondsey. It would have taken half the time if we had stayed north of the river and went London City Airport. I reckon the bastards did it on purpose to mess with my head. It bloody well worked as well because as we drove through my manor of south Bermondsey I started getting all kinds of flashbacks in my head. I used to run through these roads just a few months previous whilst training for the ABA's. we even went past the spot at Jamaica Road where I came off my motorbike a couple of years earlier. But it was when we drove past our old second floor flat on the Kirby Estate and seeing people standing outside our old shops that I thought to myself, 'will I ever see this place again? At that moment I would have given anything to be in that piss stinking lift on the Kirby.

The journey from the Bailey to Belmarsh seemed like it took forever. Once we had arrived, much like Brixton we were booked in. The big difference was HMP Belmarsh was that it was a high security prison and the largest in London, so registration was a far more grueling and stressful experience compared to Brixton. We were photographed, finger printed, had all personal items confiscated. The strip search crossed just about every boundary of common decency ever written into law in my opinion. This was followed up by psychiatric interviews, medical investigations and cell allocations. It is also worth mentioning that while we are all being assessed, this is taking place in a cage like pen full of at least 35 other newly sentenced inmates, all screaming and shouting like animals at the zoo. The moods of this new intake ranged from the despondent to the desperate.

I will never forget that day, it was June 8, I remember there was a young black prisoner, who kept ramming his head into the bars of the cage like a man possessed until his head split open. As he was being restrained and put in a strait jacket, there was blood absolutely everywhere. At the same time a very excitable young man tried to escape, which was a bit silly considering he was in the highest security prison in the UK. That was not the end of the drama because on the other side of the cage several robbery gang members were fighting amongst themselves because one of the gang got the script of his evidence wrong, which secured guilty verdicts for them all. I thought to myself, 'fucking hell, welcome to Belmarsh'.

Eventually, I was allocated a cell and sent off to House Block 3, which I quickly discovered was nicknamed Lebanon, because the block was full of 'Toolmen'(gunmen). By now I just wanted to get my head down, it had been long day and don't mind admitting I was mentally and physically drained. But there was no such luck for me as my arrival at Belmarsh had been reported on the evening news bulletin. There were no tv's in the cells in those days but there was in the gym, the food hall and the recreation areas, so word spread fast.

And, as if the day could not get any worse, I soon discovered that I was being banged up in a three man cell. I will never forget thinking as I walked through that cell door, 'Fucking hell, three men shitting in the same cell'. There was one sink, one bed, bunk beds and a toilet. Believe me when I say there was no room to stretch your legs out, I mean it, and I was shade over 5ft 4 and about six stone wet through. I put my bedding down and got my new Belmarsh regulation toothbrush

97

out. That was a waste of time because half the bloody bristles fell out in my mouth. I couldn't wait until the first canteen day so I could get new toiletries. I went back to my bed and sat back just as my two young cellmates were about to wake up. I wouldn't mind but it was only 3pm in the afternoon and they have just woken up.

This is what prison life does to you, they were only in their 30's as well. They obviously knew I had just come from court because the first thing they asked was, 'have you got any gear? I looked at them said, "what you mean, gear? "You know cannabis, brown, heroin". I said no, and with that one of the lads produced some tin fil and said, 'this is the best way to get through your time in here'. Then he brought out the brown and before he could do whatever he does with it I had kicked it out of his hand, smashed him on the edge of his chin and he was asleep before he hit the ground. Soon as he hit the deck the other lad had hit the bell and about six screws came flying in through the door and slammed me up against the wall.

The tin foil was still on the floor and one of the screws shouted, "Who's tin foil is this? I said, "it's not mine but if you leave me in this cell with these two smackheads a minute longer, I will be up for two more murders. Move me to a drug free wing. Test, do whatever you like but just get me away from these two". The head screw told me to 'calm down, we will move you to a single cell'. So that's what they did, they moved me to Spur 3 on house block 3. I think they messed up putting me in a three man cell because as Cat A prisoner I should have been in a single cell.

Believe me, if you are in the unfortunate position of being detained at Her Majesty's pleasure then a single cell is definitely the way to go. By now it was six o'clock and time for dinner, if you could call it that. As I walked down to the Spur towards the serving area, I picked up a metal tray and walked down the line. Normally you get three choices but on your court day you don't get a choice. I had to make do with some Vegetarian slop and two slices of bread followed by Rice Pudding. You get a breakfast pack for the morning which included some long life milk.

On the way back to the cell a man shouts over, 'I know you you're from Bermondsey? I replied, 'yes that's right'. Then somebody shouts, 'anything you need Pete, let me know? I was told you were coming'. It is true what they, news travels faster inside those four walls than the bloody internet. As I settled down to my first night at Belmarsh people were shouting out all around and playing loud music. The only thing on my mind at this point, though, was what was going to happen in court in eight weeks' time. Was I going to be advised to go for a not guilty plea and was my dad ok. Of course, I was in jail physically but mentally I was still at home going about my business. Morning soon came and I made some Rice Krispies with that horrible long life milk that made breakfast taste like Cement. But it filled a hole. At 10am an announcement was made to put your bell on if you wanted to go out to the exercise yard. I put my light on and a screw opened the door. 'I hear you're a bit handy with your hands McDonagh? He said. "If you leave me alone there will be no need to find out", I replied. "I just want to keep my head down, get a not guilty and go home to my family". Like all places of work, you get good and bad. Anyway, I got out and into the yard and just had a little jog round and a stretch out. I quickly noticed there were loads of little firms taking up different parts of the yard. Someone came up to me, introduced himself and said he was a friend of my brother, Liam. 'Just let me know what you need and I'll get it for you,' he said. I told him I just need some toiletries and a phone card and he said, 'no problem, I'll speak to a screw and get it to you, let me know where your cell is? I told him some wanker of a screw tried to wind me up today. My brother's friend knew exactly who I was talking about. There were two screws standing by the gate and I said that's one of them, there. "That's Mr. Rowe, he's a real Jobs worth but Mr. Jones next to him is as good as gold. I will tell you who's ok and who isn't. you're on basic at the moment so just keep your head down.

"After a few weeks you can be get more visits and get a job. I'm on the hot plate, pays £15 a week. Cleaner get £10.' I soon settled in and my new pal working on the hot plate meant I was getting a decent portion size of everything if I wanted it, even if it did taste like shit most of the time. Most afternoons we would get Association which meant we could play pool, have a shower or play cards. I was pretty good at pool so many a time I went back to my cell with a handful of Jammy Dodgers or a bar of chocolate. No drugs for me but I had plenty of sugar for my energy levels and quite a few phone cards, so I could speak to my family whenever I wanted.

My first visit at Belmarsh was a closed one, which meant it was behind glass. My brother Liam and his wife Jean came to see me but for some reason Liam was stopped from seeing me by security. Apparently, the sniffer dog took a dislike to Liam and he was not allowed to see me so it was just Jean. I asked her how my dad and Liam were and that they were not to worry. I said my good byes to Jean and went back to my Cell. When you are on remand you can have more visits but for some reason all my visits for a good couple of weeks were closed visits so when friends and family came to see me they were getting messed about or sent away without seeing me. In the end I refused to go on visits. At the time it seemed to me like I was getting the treatment. I cannot say if it was the police or the screws but it was not normal. I was looking forward to those visits and many a time I felt like kicking off but I knew I had to keep my cool and my head down. One thing boxing teaches you is self-discipline, especially under pressure. Believe me my boxing training came in very handy when it came to keeping a cool head.

Once things settled down a bit, things changed and I was allowed three open visits a week. Quite what changed I do not know but I did not care because at long last I could finally see my friends and family in a nice canteen environment with plenty of chocolate and drinks. When Liam came to see me, I asked him if dad would come along next time but he said dad was too upset to see me. Liam said he had not gone to bed since I had been in here, he just slept in the armchair. "Dad said he's not going to bed until 'my Pete comes home', said Liam. It really broke my heart hearing that but I told Liam, "Tell dad the bed is really comfortable and not to worry because the Queen is looking after me".

I cannot say I pleased at being banged up, far from it, but as well as the open visits I then got a job on the hot plate which meant I was getting more time out of my cell. I was about four weeks in at this point when a screw came up to and asked if I wanted my Codefendant to bunk in with me. I thought, 'that's a bit strange'. Was someone trying to set us up? Was the cell bugged? You have a lot of time to think in prison and I was thinking of just about everything. In any case I was innocent and my Co D was not even there so it would have been a waste of time. I said to the screw, "do me a favor gov, can you bang him up with Tez on

2's? Tez was on the cleaning roster and a good lad. He did not do drugs and I knew he would look out for him.

My next court day was scheduled exactly eight weeks after I arrived at Belmarsh. It was back to the Old Bailey, and again with a police escort and again, was left in a holding cell for what seemed like forever. My Barrister came to inform me he was applying for bail again. Once I did eventually walk the steps into court with my other three co D's I quickly found my dad, Liam, Jean and Martin sitting nervously in the public gallery. When the judge asked us all to make a plea, we all responded individually speaking clearly, NOT GUILTY. Yet again we all got refused bail so it was back to Belmarsh but not before I called out to my dad to tell him Belmarsh was like a holiday camp and that I was ok. Despite the rest of my family shaking their heads in disbelief I did manage to put a smile on his face, so it put me a bit more at ease.

Once we got back to Belmarsh I was just about to settle in when my co D came into my cell and asked if I he could come in with me. The last thing I wanted was to lose my single cell but I could see he was struggling and I really felt for him. He never said so but I could see that he was a duck out of water being banged up. I'm not saying I was an old hand at doing a bit of porridge, it was my first time inside as well. But I treated it a lot like a boxing routine by focusing and maintaining my discipline. Anyway, I agreed to end my single cell occupancy and I am glad I did because we ended up having a great laugh and the time started to fly by.

I'm nothing if not a survivor. One day I showed my co D how to make toast. He said, "But Peter we have not got a toaster so how are we going to have toast? I told him to lift up the mattress on my bed. There was a solid metal squares at the base of the bed. I would put the bread on metal base and light a match underneath. I toasted both sides with the lighted match and within a short while we would have a lovely bit of toast. I also showed him how to keep a radio working if the batteries ran out by hooking a wire up to the light fixing. It was a case of doing anything to make our lives easier, and to survive. I cannot remember the exact time but I think I had been in prison for a about four months by now. We had just had breakfast when the cell door opens and a screw walked in and told my co D to gather up his belongings. "Where are we going? He asked, hesitantly. "You're going home lad". Quick as a flash I said. "What about me, Gov? "You're not going anywhere McDonagh," replied the screw.

To say I was gutted is a huge understatement but I was really happy for my co D. As I said earlier, he was not even with us when that incident took place on Christmas Eve so he should not have even been banged up, let alone in a top security prison like Belmarsh. That boy could not have moved out of that cell quick enough. In fact, he left so quick he left me all his belongings, which of course I appreciated. I was not on my own for long, though, because no sooner had I shut the cell door to savior a bit of peace and quiet, than it opened again and another inmate came marching in to take up residence. This time it was an old boy, who had looked like he was an old hand staying at Her Majesty's pleasure. I called him K. Obviously not his real name but that's what I called him. He was on trial at the Bailey and was looking at about 25 years if he got a guilty. Because he was on trial, he was up nearly every morning and back late in the afternoon so it was not too bad. I did try and write letters but because I'm Dyslexic it was very difficult, that's why I drew lots of pictures to help my friends and family understand what I was trying to write. I used to draw things like me looking out of my cell window or overlooking the exercise yard. Anything I was writing about, really.

After about four weeks my new cell mate failed to return to the cell. When I asked the screw where K was, he said, 'he's gone home, got a not guilty'. I was really pleased because he must have been in his 60's and if he had got a guilty the chances are he would have died in prison. I felt like a bit of a lucky Leprechaun because that was the second time my cellmate had got a result and walked off home. Surely it had to be my turn soon. By now I had been in Belmarsh for five months and still no sign of a trial date.

On the upside, if ever there is one, banged up in prison I did have time to reflect. I don't mind admitting I learned a lot about myself during that time and it is definitely one place where you can find yourself. So, from that point of view that time of my life did give me time to work out where I was going in my life and where I wanted to be in the near future. I did have a little bit of good news, though, because my single cell became available again on the spur so I managed to get up there and see two of my close friends. The rest of the people on that wing were too busy chasing the Brown and anything else they could get their hands on.

Chapter 21
A VIP arrives at Belmarsh.

As you can imagine there is not much excitement goes on in prison but every now and again something happens and there is a little bit of a buzz around the place, for a short while at least. By this time, I had worked my way up to No.1 on the Hot plate which means I serve the main course at meal times, so I'm first in line. Once we had finished serving dinner, we all used to sit sat down and watch TV. We just happened to be watching the local news when a breaking story popped up to say the famous author and MP Jeffery Archer had just been found guilty of perjury and perverting the course of justice, and was on his way to Belmarsh. I could only have imagined how different it must have been for him to spend the night in Belmarsh after the privileged life he had lived up until then. It was certainly a bit different than holding court in the House of Commons.

Once we had a chance to digest the imminent arrival of our VIP, a screw came over and said, "McDonagh, when Jeffery Archer arrives you will be serving him dinner. As I was No.1 on hot plate duty, I suppose it made sense.

I remember it like it was yesterday. Jeffery came up to the hot plate wearing blue trousers and a tweed like shirt. He reminded me of my old Co D, He looked nervous and kept his head down. I cannot say I blame him as he had just been thrust into a life far removed from the one that he had previously been used to. He was the last person you would expect to see at Belmarsh. When a prisoner comes in from court so late in the day, they do not get a choice of what to eat. Its normally A on the menu or nothing. A is the slops. After each day you need to fill out a sheet of what food has been used so if anything is left over it goes on menu A, so for any inmate coming in from court at the end of the day the food really must taste like shit. I could see Jeffery had had a hard day. I said to him, "mate, what do you want? He said, 'could I have that Chicken? I think it was C on the menu. The screw said, 'no, it's A for him'. I gave him A but also slipped a bit of Chicken on his tray as well. The screw saw what I did but just smiled and turned a blind eye

There is not any one look a prisoner has as the penal system is full of people from all walks of life, and pretty much no one looks that much out of place. But I have to say Jeffery Archer was very much an exception to the rule. Maybe, knowing he was a Lord and an MP made him look out of place.

I did try and make Jeffery feel more comfortable and more relaxed. It did not matter who it was, famous author or some young kid inside for the first time. I had only been in prison for five months myself but I was lucky I learnt on the job and was strong enough, mentally. In my little time there I had seen people slit their wrists, a man swallowed a razor blade and young kid try and hang himself in the cell next to me. I was really not trying to be some kind of do gooder but I would always go out of my way to help someone if I thought it made life easier for them.

After a couple of days, it looked like Jeffery was settling in a bit and was more relaxed. When he came up to the hot plate for his lunch, he asked me if there was any chance, he I could get someone to wash and Iron a shirt and trousers for him as his wife was coming up to visit in a couple of days' time. First thing that ran through my mind was my dad as I always wanted to show him, I was ok and not to worry. Obviously, I could not read Jeffery's mind but it looked to me as though he wanted his wife to also know that he was ok as well. I was happy to help so I said, "no problem, mate, I will come up and collect your clothes after lunch". As promised, I went up to his cell, picked up the clothes and arranged for the laundry man to wash and iron everything he needed. The next day I picked up his clothes and delivered them
104

back to him. As everyone was on association all the cell doors were open so I just knocked, walked in. He had his back to me and was writing. I said, "there you go mate, your laundry has arrived". As he turned around, he looked at me down his glasses and politely said, 'thank you'. I did say that I fully understood it was important to look smart on visiting days. Jeffery then asked if he could mention me in his book. I said of course he could. Until he mentioned it, I had no clue he was an author, let alone a famous one. Of course, I knew he was a lord and a former MP because of all the publicity but I honestly did not have a clue he was a famous writer.

At that point I was a little bit in awe of him. Not because of who he was but because he could write. I could not even bloody well read, let alone write. As I said earlier, I am Dyslexic and, in those days, there was not much understanding of Dyslexia so I was never really encouraged or helped to learn to read, so I never even tried. I told Jeffery that I never really went to school and he said, 'the only way to get knowledge is to read'. I then explained that I could not read and he quickly countered by saying, "well you have plenty of time to learn to read in here". He gave me some advice of what books I needed to have to learn and said when you do start reading, always make sure it is something you are interested in because reading is a lot easier when you have an interest in something. Before I knew it, I way flying with the reading and it was all down to him. I will never forget the advice he gave me that day in his cell and will never repeat it, but he really helped me through some hard times and has been a real inspiration. That advise has inspired me to write this book. One thing I will share, though, is Jeffery did say, "when you do write a book, write it in your own words, no one else can put the emotions and feelings into a book better than the person who is the subject. People will understand, who you really are." He was only in Belmarsh for a short time and he was not treated any differently than anyone else, in fact he was probably treated worse. While he was there, we spoke quite a bit about family, friends, education, even a bit of sport as well. I have to say, though, Jeffery Archer is a man of his word because he did mention me in his book and it was nice to have made an impact in someone's life no matter how big or small. If I had never met Jeffery, I do not think I would be writing my life story now.

Twenty years later I have taken his advice and written this book in my own words, not anyone else's, mine.

Chapter 22
Trial date approaches

I had now been incarcerated in Belmarsh for nearly six months but at long last my trial date had been set for three months' time. Up until now, apart from my first day being banged up with two smackheads, I had managed to keep my nose clean and out of trouble. Belmarsh, like all prisons I imagine, is a funny place in the sense that one minute there is complete silence and the next it kicks off and erupts for no reason. Drug usage and screws winding up inmates was a massive factor in fights breaking out. It did not matter where it was, the gym, football matches in the exercise yard, there was always something. As long as no one said anything to me I was happy and knowing I only had three months until my trial I was doubly determined to keep my nose clean and my head down. The way I saw it was, every day was getting closer to my trial date and me getting home.

As my trial date got closer and closer, I had a legal visit from my Junior Barrister. The trial was going to be at the Old Bailey, where I had had my initial bail hearings. One thing I did know, though, was after sharing a cell with the old boy K, the trial days were going to be long. The day would probably start between 5am and 6am and not finish from anything up to 7pm. There was never a set routine when it came to being driven to court, for security reasons in case someone was watching the timings in and out to plan a possible breakout from the prison van. During the meeting with the Barrister, I did ask how my chances were looking. He just looked straight at me, no messing about and said," It is going to be a tough case". I then replied back equally as stern and said, "what is worst outcome? "For attempted murder you could get life but that will be hard to prove. It could be GBH section 18 with intent. If you go not guilty you could get 12 years". After that legal visit I quickly came to the conclusion that I may as well make myself comfortable here because I could be spending quite a long time at Her Majesty's pleasure. Until that meeting with the Barrister, I was pretty upbeat that justice was going to prevail when I had my day in court. Of course, I was nervous and being honest, pretty much afraid of what was happening to me at times. But on hearing that news my head just raced ahead and mentally I was not in a good place. Even worse was I remember Liam telling me how my dad was sleeping in the armchair in front of the tv every night and was not going to go to bed until he had me home with him. I now understand what people mean when they say, 'I can handle this situation but I just worry about how the loved ones around me will cope'. And it is true because I was more worried about how my family, Tish, Liam, Martin, my dad, were going to cope if I was found guilty and sentenced to life imprisonment. I had visions of going to my dad's funeral in handcuffs and having to endure my siblings watch me being carted off back to prison. I was trying to not be negative but I had to picture every scenario and face every possible outcome.

When I got back to the Wing, I had a chat with a few of the lads and told them about my pre trial meeting. I told them I could be looking at life imprisonment or if I am lucky, 12 years. They just said that I had to be positive and stay focused on the trial. That is exactly what I did. For the next five weeks until the trial I read every single word of the 4,000 word case file, back to back over and over again, picking out flaws in witness and police statements, and making sure my brief, fully understood everything I wanted him to do and say. I have Jeffery Archer to thank because when I arrived at Belmarsh eight months earlier my reading was under fives Ladybird book standard at best, but now I was becoming a connoisseur of the written word-by my standards, anyway.

The first day of the trial soon arrived and I was up at 5am and suited and booted. It took about two hours to march me through the prison, put the cuffs on and put me in the sweat box. For all the messing about to get me in the van at Belmarsh, it took all of five or 10 minutes to get me parked up at the Bailey. Like I said earlier, you feel like royalty being rushed through the centre of London with a police escort driving through, with all the red lights blazing. By now I was getting to know the routine so I pretty much directed myself to the holding cell. Luckily for me, I was not held for too long before I was called up to attend Court 13 on the ground floor. I could quite easily have thought, 'shit, unlucky 13', but I was past all that superstitious stuff by now. Afterall, how much bad luck can one man have?

I have to say, at this point, walking into that dock and then seeing the judge, the legal teams and all those jurors about to be sworn in, completely took me aback. It was one thing walking into the dock at the Bailey for a bail hearing but a full trial? It suddenly dawned on me; this is as fucking serious as it gets. For those that have never been involved in a Crown court trial, one of the first things to happen is the jury need to be sworn in. At this time the defendant or his prosecution team can request whether or not they are happy or not with the choice of jury. The judge also asks the jury members if they know any of the defendants on trial. Both of these things happened this time because one of my team was not happy with the choice of a particular juror and another one said they knew me. So, whilst the jury situation was being sorted out, we were taken back to the holding cells.

I will never forget that pokey little cell. Trust me it was small, cold and it stunk of just about anything you could possibly imagine, only worse. They may as well have thrown me back in the sweat box. Not long after, I was brought back to the cell my barrister came in said 'one of your co defendants has gone guilty'. I said, "to attempted murder? He replied, 'No, He's done a deal. He will plead guilty to section 11 GBH. I then asked, "how long would he get? The barrister paused for a second and said, "he could still get life but that is unlikely as he has gone guilty and saved the court considerable time and money.

Now, there was only two of us left so the trial time was greatly reduced. The barrister also mentioned that I had been offered the same deal. I did take a brief moment to think about things but I knew I had not done anything wrong so I said, "No, I'm not guilty". There was never any question of me pleading guilty to something I had not done but I had to have a brief think to weigh things up. "good", said the barrister," because we have a very good case. I am now going to go and have some legal arguments over some evidence.

I eventually found out that the legal argument in question was that the prosecution wanted to use evidence in court that had been obtained by bugging devices that had been planted in various places. Apparently, prosecution legal teams had tried to use this method of evidence in the past but had always been refused. My legal team and the prosecution argued over the legalities for two days until day three when the judge came to a decision that the evidence could be used. I was told at the time that history was being made because this was the first time a covert listening device was allowed to be submitted as evidence in a UK court of law. Regardless of whether it was true or not the fact was, it was another obstacle my legal team had to deal with. After nine months the trial eventually got underway. On the very first day, I looked up to the public gallery and I could see how much the effect this trial was having on all of my family. They tried to be strong for me but I could see, especially on my dad's face, that the worry of what could happen to me was affecting him. It was one of those trials where I thought it was going well one day and not so good the next. I would go back to my cell in the evening and think, 'that went well today'. Then the day after I would come back, lay on my bunk and thought, 'this could be my home for the next few years'. Especially when some witnesses and murder squad detectives blatantly lied in open court before getting found out. As I said when the trial was going well the weekends flew by but when it did not, a couple of days felt like a week.

Eventually, the 10 week trial was coming to an end and it was time for the summing up. I'm not trying to be clever here but for those that are not familiar with Crown Court proceedings, summing up is basically a much shortened version of what came out in the trial. The prosecution presents their reasoning of why the defendant is guilty and the defence will plead for the innocence of their client. The judge then balances up both versions and directs the jury on points of law that should be taken into account or disregarded. I say the judge balances up both versions of what was said during the trial but after hearing what he had to say about me I certainly did not feel the scales of justice were evenly balanced.

Having said that, during the summing up my barrister did read out character references from my boxing coach Steve Hiser and my local MP Simon Hughes, which definitely instilled me with some renewed confidence. But the fact remained I was on trial for attempted murder, GBH Section 18 with intent, GBH and Affray. And there were 12 jurors, who were tasked with whether or not I go home to my family that night and continue my life as a free man, or spend what could be at least 10 years behind the door of one of London's outdated and over populated prisons.

I remember it very clearly. It was a Thursday afternoon around 2pm when the judge finished summing up, at which time the jury were dismissed to consider their verdict. As the hours of business at Crown Court finish around 4.30pm it was safe to say that a verdict was not going to be reached. I thought I was going to be taken to that shitty smelly single cell but instead I was thrown into a larger holding cell with about five other defendants, all, like me, waiting for verdicts. You could hear a pin drop in that cell, no one said a bloody word for at least 10 minutes. I cannot say I was surprised because we were all too busy worrying about where we were sleeping that night. It was that quiet I could hear the key in the lock turn. It was 4pm now and the screw comes in and shouted, 'Right, everyone back to Belmarsh'.

I never slept a wink that night. I was only 23 years old, and if you have got this far in the book you know that so far, my life has been filled with mixed emotions, sadness and huge disappointments. The two constants that had always kept me going and on the straight and narrow up until now was the love of my family, and my boxing. I can honestly say lying in bed that night, for the first time in my life, I could understand why some people harbour thoughts of either suicide or self harm. I really was at rock bottom that night, in particular because, not only were 12 people I had never met in a position to decide my future, but I had let my family down, especially my dad. He had been through hell with the way my mother treated him. And he had sacrificed everything to bring up us kids, and this was how I was repaying him.

On the Friday morning I had people asking how the trial was going and wishing me good luck. Listening to everyone telling me to stay positive gave me a bit of a lift. I was back in court at 9am and put in the holding cell again with the same people I was with the day before. Again, I remember the time exactly, it was 11am when the screw came in and shouted out, 'McDonagh'. It was time to go, and again my stress levels reached maximum thinking 'this is it'. So, there I go, walking down the dark narrow corridor thinking a verdict has been reached and all it was, was the Jury wanted to asked a question. Once my barrister had given his answer, I was marched back to the holding cell. Again, if you are not familiar with how the system works, once a jury is out, if there are any questions to be asked at all, the defendant always has the right to be in court to hear the answer. When I did get back to the cells the other lads were sitting there with their heads in their hands. One looked up and said 'Guilty or not guilty? I just told him there was only a question from the jury that needed answering. I noticed a couple of the other lads were missing so asked where they were. Someone said the jury had reached a verdict in their case about half hour ago. With that the cell door came flying open and in they walked looking like they had seen a ghost. One of the lads sat down, just before he fell down. 'I'm never going to see my kids again' he said, while the other one threw up all over the floor. The first lad then says,' we're fucked, two murder charges and lifted off'. They were both moved out very quickly. This was no tv drama, the reality of what had just happened to those two lads left us in no doubt what fate could be awaiting the rest of us. To make matters worse the jury could not reach a verdict on Friday, so myself and my co D were sent back to Belmarsh for the weekend. Believe me that weekend felt like a year. My emotions were all over the
111

place. My mind was racing at 100 miles an hour, what if I am guilty, what if they can't come to a verdict, what if a juror falls ill and there has to be a retrial? Then I thought about my family, how will they cope? I was an absolute mess and the worse thing of all was, I was totally bloody innocent. I never ate a thing or slept the entire weekend, and was glad when Monday morning arrived and was told to get ready for court. It was one of those things where I was dreading having to face the judge in court but at the same time just wanted it to be over with. On the positive side I did write a note saying that if I do go home today I wanted all my belongings to go to my mate Johnny. Sounds daft as we never had a lot but when you are inside a radio, canteen and phone cards as well as toiletries are excellent currency to exchange. Johnny was suffering mentally. He was a nice man and he never had any visits that I knew and no one ever wrote to him to my knowledge, so I knew that small gesture would mean the world to him.

On the way to court I was really hoping that the jury had a great weekend because I wanted this over with quick and of course, in my favour. This time instead of being in Court 13 we were directed to Court 1. I said earlier that I was not superstitious when it came to numbers but when I heard we had swerved Court 13 I thought, 'that's handy, maybe it's an Omen'. I was right because soon after hearing the court room change, the Clerk of the court came into the cells and told me the jury had reached a verdict. This really was squeaky bum time because as much as I wanted this nightmare to be over, part of me was numb with fear. I remember walking along that narrow half lit corridor and up the steps to the dock and thinking 'I know what it must have been like now for all those infamous prisoners of the past like the Yorkshire Ripper and Dennis Nilsen to face justice inside the most famous court in the country.

My co D was already in the dock. I was told not to face the jury. What I'm going to say now is going to sound as if I'm a sandwich short of a picnic but I swear this is how I remember it. Whether my mind was playing tricks with me or the thought of my life flashing before me triggered something off I do not know but both seats next to me were

112

empty. I suddenly felt something on my shoulder. I had a friend called Nicky and he had a 14 year old sister that had died of cancer. To my shock, as clear as day she was sitting there smiling at me and said, 'don't worry you're getting a not guilty'. I swear, I looked at my Co D and said, 'I bet we get a not guilty'.

I'm now looking directly at the jury when the judge asks the foreman of the Jury to stand up. 'Have you reached a verdict on which at least a majority of 10-2 have agreed in the case of Peter McDonagh? said the judge. 'Yes, my lord,' was the prompt reply. 'On the first count of attempted murder, what is the verdict? 'Not Guilty'. 'On the second count of GBH Section 18 with intent? 'Not guilty'. On the third count of GBH? 'Not guilty'. 'On the fourth count of Affray? 'Not guilty'.

Aa soon as that fourth not guilty was read out I could see my family in the public gallery jumping up and down, cuddling each other. The relief in my dad's eyes was there for everyone to see. I had not seen him so happy in years. As far as I was concerned that was it, I was ready to walk there and then but I was stopped in my tracks as paperwork had to be signed to make sure there were no other pending charges. I had waited nearly a year to be found innocent so another few minutes was not going to hurt. My co D, who was also found not guilty, and me were taken back to the cells to prepare for release. Back in the cells emotions were running high because it was only a 10 metre by 10 metre space and there were at six of us in there, some were found guilty and looking at years in prison and there was me walking out the door in a matter of minutes. Five minute later someone else comes in shouting 'I've been found guilty'. It really was a mixture of emotions so when I was called to be released, I just could not look back knowing some of those men were never seeing daylight again. As I was marched through the final remaining gate to freedom the screw said, 'this is it McDonagh, the other side of this gate is freedom'. I just smiled and said, 'Thank fuck for that'. Believe me, the air on the other side of that gate smelt far fresher than anything I had smelt for a long time. I felt a little odd for a few moments to be mixing with the public again, but at the same time, sheer relief because I was once again breathing free air as a free man. That is until one of the murder squad detectives brushed past me and said," you were lucky this time, see you on the next one". Quick as a flash I replied, "Your never gonna see me again".

Chapter 23
Freedom at last

Until you have had your liberty taken away you have no idea the effect it can have, not only on your physical health but also your mental health as well. I will never forget how happy I was to see my dad, brothers, and Jean waiting outside the court for me. There were cameras and reporters everywhere but all I was interested in was being with my family and breathing air again as a free man. By this time Tish was living back in Ireland with her family but she was on the phone when I came out, so I had a quick chat with her and promised I will be over to visit her very soon. Everything seemed like it was moving at a 100mph, even in the taxi home I had to ask the driver to slow down. Those black Taxis are not exactly known for their speed but I had been in prison for nine months and it was just moving along too quick.

Once we got over Tower Bridge and hit Bermondsey it finally sunk in that I was actually going home. The first thing I did was go straight to my local pub where there was about 300 people waiting for me. I drank so much Guinness that night but I was not drunk because everyone was asking what it was like in there and I was too busy talking to feel under the influence. I went home that night and my dad and me stayed up to the early hours talking. That's when he told me he had not slept in his bed all the time I was in prison. He just fell asleep in the chair. "You can sleep in your own bed tonight I'm home now". He just smiled and said, "I think I need to; don't you dare get in trouble with the police again".

I gave myself a few weeks to get myself together again before going back down the Fisher to start boxing again. I could not wait to get back and start training. I had put on a bit of weight again so I was a bit worried about my coach Steve and what he might have to say.

When I did get back to the Fisher and started training hard again it just did not feel right. I think I needed a break so decided to go to Ireland and spend some time with Tish and her family. I did not realise at the time but my mind was just all over the place and I needed to get away to sort myself out. I phoned Tish and told her 'I'm coming to stay with you in Ireland'. She said that was fine, 'but what are you gonna do? I said I would get a job. So, the next day I went back up the Fisher and told Steve I was taking time away to sort my head out. I said the same thing to my dad and both agreed it was the best thing to do. It was tough leaving my dad in Bermondsey but he knew it was best for me at this time of my life.

Stepping off that plane and landing on Irish soil felt really good. It was as if a massive weight had been lifted off my shoulders. There was a lot going on inside my head at the time. Being locked up for for something I knew I did not do, worrying about how my family were coping, having to miss the ABA's, it all took a massive toll on my mental health. I knew running away was not going to fix things but I needed to be in a different environment for a while and to decide what I wanted to do with my life. And of course, it was great to spend time with Tish again and my little nephew.

While I was on the bus from Dublin Airport to Galway and Carraroe, which was a good four hour bus ride, I did think about my life in Bermondsey but as soon as we got to travel along the West Atlantic coast by the sea to Carraroe, I realised how beautiful and picturesque my homeland really is. I have to say, I was not unhappy living in Bermondsey, but Ireland was home and the place I was born.

I mentioned earlier that once my mum had left us all those years ago, Tish took on the parental responsibilities because she was the oldest and Dad was busy out working hard to keep a roof over our heads and food on the table. So, it was no surprise to me that soon after I arrived Tish had announced that she had lined me up a job in the local factory.

115

I will never forget it; I was making binders and folders. It was not the best job in the world but at least I was earning a wage and the people there were really nice. After a while I felt like I was getting back to my old self but I was now missing my boxing so to fill the void I started going to the local pub. It was getting to the point where I was in the pub pretty much every night of the week. This went on for a good few months and as you can imagine Tish was starting to give me a hard time about as well. She sat me down and told me straight, "Peter, this is not a good life for you. Boxing makes you happy, go back to London and start boxing again? She was right I did miss my boxing but maybe not in the way a normal person would. Maybe this is something only some other boxers can relate to, but what I think I was missing was being punched in the face. It was like a form of self harming, like self punishment. Whatever the reason was I missed boxing.

Tish was right, I had always intended to go back to London and start boxing again but the turning point for me came when I was on the way home from the pub one night. Tish's house was about 10 miles away from the pub so that meant I had to drive. In Ireland, especially out in the country, the police used to put barricades up to stop people drink and driving and to check whether or not the driver had insurance. This particular night I had drunk about 10 pints of Guinness so I drove straight through the barricade and flipped the car clean over on to its roof and into a bog. A bog is a piece of land where you collect turf to burn on fires. Luckily for me I was ok and nobody else was around. The first thing I thought was, 'I have to get out of here and make a run for it'. The police must have thought I was dead at first but by the time they got to the car I was out and running into the next field. There were blue flashing lights everywhere. I did manage to climb over a few fences and across gardens to reach some open land and get away. I had just bought this Peugeot 205 so again, luckily for me I had not registered it yet. The car was still registered at the seller's address.

It was really late by the time I got home and Tish was in bed. So, I jumped in the shower and went straight to bed. In the morning Tish came into my room and said, "Pete, where's your car? I told her I had left it at the pub because I had had too much to drink last night. I told her I did not feel that well so was not going into work. "That's because you had too much beer last night," she said. "I know your hiding something Pete," she argued. I should have known I could not fool Tish; she knew me better than I knew myself so I came clean. "I drove through a police road block last night, Tish. "I'm lucky to be alive. Turned the car over. It landed in a bog upside down. I had to do a runner as I had a few too many to drink".

Tish did not mince her words, "Your gotta go back to London Peter, if you don't you will end up like Mum". "I bloody won't end up like her", I said. Tish knew I did not like amateur boxing anymore, which is why she shouted at me. "Well then go back and stay with Dad, get back to your boxing and contact some professional promoters and make something of your life. Because if you stay here you will end up like a sad old drunk".

I spent the next week contemplating on what to do next. I was really struggling. I knew Tish was right but I just had to get my head round it. Twenty years there was not the help and understanding of mental illness like there is today. I'm not for one minute saying it is perfect now, but at least help is out there in some form. Back then we were just encouraged to snap out of it and crack on. After much thought and thinking about what Tish had said I decided to quit my job and go back to London. But not before I had one last session at the local pub. It was a Friday night and the reason I went was to see my Godfather, Porick. The last time I had seen him I remember saying that I was going back to England, turn professional and win the Irish boxing title. I needed to remind him of what I said. I must admit he looked at me is if I was mad because in the same breath I said, 'Come on, let's go to the local nightclub'. But I insisted, "I promise you, Poreck, I will make, you, and all the family proud by bringing the Irish title back the Connemara."

That was a heavy night I can tell you and I could not even remember getting home to my sister's on the Saturday morning. I remember Tish

117

coming into my room and saying, "same old story then, I suppose you were out drinking last night? "I was yes, but this is the last time because I'm going back to London tomorrow. I'm booking a flight back to Gatwick, I'm gonna take your advice and I'm going to turn professional. I've told Poreck I'm turning pro, win the Irish title and make you proud".

I was sad to leave my home town but it was something I really needed to do because Tish was right, I was one drink away from becoming a drunk. The whole idea of me going to Ireland in the first place was to straighten myself out but the drinking was only making my mental health worse. Once I had made up my mind, I made a quick exit. Apart from Tish and my little nephew I did not say good bye to anybody, I just got on that plane and never looked back.

Chapter 24

Turning pro and learning the game

When I got back to London, I spent a week or so with my dad and brothers, and catching up with my friends again. I was in a better frame of mind now because although I was drinking a bit too much, I was in Ireland and I think I needed it to get it out of my system after spending so much time at Her Majesty's pleasure. Also, after missing out on the ABA's due to my incarceration- in my sub conscious-I always knew I was going to turn professional. First thing I did was call local promoter Eugene Maloney, the brother of Frank Maloney, who at the time was a very well connected boxing promoter. Frank later became Kellie Maloney but that is another story.

A couple of days before I called Eugene, I went down the Fisher to let Steve Hiser know my plans on turning pro. Steve wished me the best of luck but said 'it was a mugs game'. I replied by saying, "Steve, I will always be grateful for what you have done for me. You have made me the man I am today but I have to do this and find my own path". Steve wished me luck but insisted on one last bit of advice. "Son, you will be on your own in the professional game, you look after yourself." That was the best advice I could have got and it was not long before I fully understood what Steve meant.

The very next day I called Eugene and the first thing he asked me was, 'how many tickets can you sell? Not, what standard did you box at? Who have you boxed for? have you won any titles? This was followed by, "this is no longer a sport, this is the pro game, it's a business". I told

Eugene I was a local Bermondsey boy and could sell plenty of tickets. Eugene then produced a contract and said you're fighting at the Elephant and Castle Leisure Centre in eight weeks. It was as simple as that. The Elephant and Castle was only a couple of miles away so I knew I could sell the place out. Once I had undergone a full medical at a Clinic in Harley Street, London, I was then granted my licence to box under the supervision of the British Boxing Board of Control.

That eight weeks soon came around and I enlisted the help of George Woodman, who was mentored by Steve down at the Fisher Club. George turned over as a pro trainer with me. Training pro seemed a little surreal because not only was I boxing 6x2 minute rounds when I thought all pro bouts were 3x3 minutes but it was also strange that I had one trainer all to myself while preparing for a bout instead of having to share him with 10 other lads. It was also very lonely at times because not only did I have to run on my own I had run twice as far. I also found out very quickly that fighting 6x2 minutes meant you did not get paid as much, which I think was a bloody liberty.

The day before my pro debut I weighed in bang on the 10st limit agreed for the bout. One of the great advantages of boxing professionally is that after the weigh in I could scoff myself silly and not worry. As an amateur you weighed in on the day and boxed soon after so quite a lot of the time all us boxers were walking around with empty bellies. As soon as the weigh in was over I rang Tish to tell her the good news and how much I was looking forward to my pro debut. I was a bit disappointed I could not get through but I had the surprise of my life when I got home to dad's because there, she was sitting there waiting for me. First thing I said to Tish was, "told I would do it". Seeing Tish there gave me a massive boost, she was always my biggest fan and she said, 'I'm so proud of you'. We then both started laughing because I did ask her if the police were still looking for me for turning my car over in the bog on my way home from the pub.

The next day, Sunday afternoon, was fight day for me. I will never forget it, it was the 28 April, 2002. I had sold 500 tickets and the whole place was buzzing. My walk to the ring was at 4pm and I honestly thought I was the man, invincible. My family were so proud, and if I'm honest, I too was proud of myself because only two months earlier I was not long out of Belmarsh and was regularly rolling out of the pub every night at all hours, pissed as a fart.

My first opponent that day was a very experienced journeyman by the name of Arv Mittoo, who had a record of 9 wins, 54 losses and 4 draws. Please do not let that record fool you. A journeyman boxer is a highly skilled practician of the noble art. They are highly skilled, know how to defend themselves and will always do enough to make a fight of it against the local ticket selling prospect, without being too lively. Arv was from Birmingham and trained out of a gym run by a real character called Norman 'Nobby' Nobbs. Nobby was always telling jokes and entertaining the crowds between rounds. I swear he could have made it as a stand up comedian but there was nothing funny about his stable of boxers, even if his gym was named 'Losers Unlimited'. Nobby had about eight or 10 boxers in his stable and they all took fights at short notice. In fact, it was considered a serious camp if they had a week's notice to prepare for a bout. To cut a long story short, Arv possessed all those qualities of the journeyman boxer, and I did box really well to win all six rounds on the referee's card. I learned so much and was made to fight for every second of the fight.

I boxed again six weeks later and won that one as well, on points against another boxer from the Nobby's gym. After two wins I was getting a reputation as a ticket seller. One day Eugene got a call from his brother Frank, who was working with the No.1 promoter at the time, Frank Warren. Warren had a contract with Sky Sports and he wanted me to fight on one of his cards that was broadcast on Sky Sports. By now I had been back from Ireland for about three months so to get on a live televised card on Sky Sports was pretty impressive for me.

Yet again, I was facing a Nobby Nobbs boxer but this time it was a massive step up for me. Peter Buckley was the ultimate journeyman. He was fast approaching 200 fights and although he only won 28 of them, he knows every trick in the book. From a sneaky elbow or head butt to rubbing the lace part of the glove in your eye, he knew them all. That's why you really learn your trade in those early fights. This time I was boxing a four rounder so it was three minute rounds. Again, I boxed well and won the decision but I learned so much once again. Peter eventually finished his career after his 300th fight and only ever failed to hear the final bell 10 times. By now the word was going around that I was suited to the pro game. Fighting on tv gave me a bit of an inflated opinion of myself if I'm honest. I was going out partying and thought I was the man. I started missing training, missing out runs. I was doing all sorts of different things like being on the front of Time Magazine, a London circulated free mag. I thought I had hit the big time after three wins but I was soon brought back down with a bump in my next fight.

It was against a kid called Ben Hudson. He was short and stocky and was a ticket seller, just like me. He was no journeyman and we had sold over 600 tickets between us, so the atmosphere at the famous York Hall in London was amazing. This was the first real fight for me because it was the first time someone was coming to fight and win and not just show a few tricks of the trade. From the first bell, Ben was like a Bull in a China shop and because I had not put the work in, I was blowing out of my arse at the end of the first round. Ben sat on my chest for the entire fight and at the end of the six rounds the decision did not go my way. No excuses, I lost fair and square. I learned two valuable lessons that night. The first one was fail to prepare, prepare to fail. The second lesson, and it was one that my amateur coach Steve had said when I told him I was turning pro. 'You will be on your own'. If Steve said that I knew to take him at his word. He was the wisest man I ever met, so I knew he was right. But I never thought I would realise his wise words so soon into my fledgling career. I had sold over 400 tickets for the fourth fight in succession but when I left the York Hall that night, there was no one anywhere to be seen. It was just me and my trainer walking out of that famous old boxing venue. Everyone loves a winner but when you're losing, no one seems to care. That's the top and bottom of it.

I know it was only my fourth pro fight, and fighters know when they have been outclassed by the better boxer, no matter what they say after losing. But I knew I had not put the work in. I had missed running sessions and I had skipped the gym, so I only had myself to blame. All I could think about was gaining revenge over 'Cat Weazle'. In fact, I was so obsessed at revenge I lost my next fight four months later. Somehow that defeat did not bother me, I just wanted the Hudson rematch. I got my wish, this time it was over four three minute rounds instead of six two's, which suited me better. Again, it was at the York Hall but I had only sold about 50 tickets while Hudson had about 400. Hudson was from Cambridge but anyone would think he was the home fighter the way his fans were cheering him on. It did not matter how many fans he had supporting him; I had done my work for this fight and there was no way he was going to beat me. I knew another defeat and that's me done. I was so focused that night I boxed beautifully. In fact I thought it was the best I had ever boxed. I'll be honest, though, I trained really hard and put the work in and won, then I would go mad and party and take my foot off the pedal.

After I got my revenge over Hudson, I left Eugene Maloney and signed with Jim Evans, a proper old school trainer/manager, who had a gym in his back garden in Maidenhead, Berkshire. Jim said he would get me a Southern Area title fight. Back in 2004 the Southern Area was a massive title as a professional. If you won that title there was a good chance you would be put forward for a British title eliminator. Lloyd Honeyghan, who boxed for my old amateur club, Fisher ABC, won the Southern Area title before becoming the undisputed welterweight champion of the world. I had also just met Candice as well, so life was good. Everything was coming together for me now. I had just met my future wife and Jim had promised to get me my first title shot. But first I had to defeat a very good boxer called Chill John in his own back yard at the Town Hall in Hove, Brighton. As you can imagine, John was really up for it. And to make matters worse, pretty much every person in the place, apart from my manager, Jim Evans, was cheering for John. I knew I was going to have to do something a little bit special if I was going to get out of that ring with a win so I had made up my mind, I was going stick it on John from the opening bell. As soon as the bell rang, I took control. It was not so much how busy I was; I just placed my shots better and every one of those punches was heavy and accurate. I knew I had hurt John with every hook to the body. I could see it on his face. So, by the end of the second round, I was not surprised when he retired with a suspected broken rib. I was so happy to get that win and the very next day, Jim, true to his word, went to work to get me a Southern Area lightweight title shot against Jon Honney, from Basingstoke.

Jon was by far my biggest test and had just taken British champion Graham Earl to the wire in a close fight, so I knew I was very much the underdog. Up until now I had always been the underdog anyway, so this was nothing new to me.

After a bit of negotiation, we managed to secure the fight for April 7, 2004 at the Equinox Nightclub in London's Leicester Square. Just like the Hudson rematch I left no stone unturned. I trained like a lunatic and was in the best shape of my life. I had only boxed a month or so before so I was fighting fit, anyway. I remember the ring walk that night like it was yesterday. The place was buzzing and I was back to selling 100's of tickets. The Equinox was not your typical boxing venue. It was, as you can imagine, how a night club would be. The place looked pretty small when it was empty but with more than 2,000 people crammed in the atmosphere was like a sold out Wembley stadium.

As I walked to the ring I remember thinking 'there is no way I'm losing tonight'. On paper this was a good trade fight as they say in boxing circles. To cut a long story short I produced the best performance of my fledgling career so far. I gave Honney a boxing lesson for at least eight of the 10 rounds to become the Southern Area lightweight champion in only my 11th fight. It was a great feeling to have my hand raised at the end and an even better feeling to see how proud Tish, my dad and the rest of the family were of me, especially after everything I had put them through.

Becoming a champion for the first time should have been the platform and motivation I needed to really push on with my boxing career and make a better life for myself and my family. But, yet again it just set me on the road to self-destruction. Pretty much all my life up until then that

124

was good, things that made me happy and smile, were either quickly taken away or turned to disappointment. I did not realise it at the time but maybe moving away from my beautiful idyllic life in Ireland to Bermondsey, the constant rejection of my mother and the trauma of being charged with attempted murder, were affecting me more than I thought. It should have felt great turning my life around and being a winner but it just set me back and had the opposite effect because I lost my next SIX fights including the Southern Area title, I was so proud of. It is difficult to explain but it was as if I was expecting things to fall apart so I let it happen before it actually did. It was a bit like self harming I suppose.

If you have got this far in the book then you will know by now that the one constant in my life so far is I have experienced more ups and downs than a ride on a Roller Coaster. And one thing you can guarantee with me is, when one door closes another one opens.

Chapter 25

Uri Geller, Fight fix allegations and a dream come true

Not long after my sixth straight defeat I got a call from my manager Jim Evans. It was around November time and I was well and truly on the source and had not even walked past a gym in two months let alone been inside one. "Pete, its Jim, are you sitting down? I might have a fight for you if you're interested? "I'm a bloody fighter Jim, of course I'm interested", I replied back. "This is a big fight and it's for a title. It's for the vacant Irish lightweight title and its against Michael Gomez, live on RTE on January 28, so no Christmas for you".

Not only was it for the Irish title, it was against a former world champion and I was a massive underdog. But on the plus side I had 12 weeks' notice and it was my dream fight. I always told Tish I would fight for the Irish title so this was a dream come true for me. Gomez was a massive puncher and it was going out live on Irish terrestrial tv in front of a million people so this was my opportunity to impress. Candice, my girlfriend at the time, was pregnant with our first child so things were definitely looking up again. I remember thinking, 'If I can get this win, it's the big time for me'.

I rang my trainer George and told him the good news. I was buzzing when I rang him and said we got an Irish title fight. George said," who you fighting? I said I didn't bloody care; it could be King Kong for all I care, I'm going to be champion of me country. "Come on McDonagh don't mess about, who is it? When I told him it was Gomez, he went quiet for a minute then said, "fuck off you're winding me up. Are you serious, he knocks people out for fun? Talk about deflating my confidence in one sentence. And he was my bloody trainer! He honestly thought there was more chance of seeing Lord Lucan riding Shergar through the Irish countryside than me beating Gomez.

Anyway, I told him camp starts on Monday and we have 12 weeks to prepare. Now this is how daft and self destructive I could be. I was about two weeks into training for the biggest fight of my career when the phone rings. It was Frank Maloney, and he sounded stressed out. I was in McDonald's at the time scoffing a Big Mac, Fries and a Milkshake. I know, I had just started camp and I was eating shit but that's another story.   It was about 3pm on a Friday and Frank says, "do you fancy a fight tonight at the York Hall, we are struggling, a fight has fallen through and Sky tv are gonna pull the live show if I can't make this fight?

I agreed to take the fight, so rushed home to Epsom, picked up my gym bag and headed round the m25. I called George on the way and told him to get down the York Hall as I was fighting tonight. He said, "are you mad you are fighting for the Irish title in 10 weeks, anything could happen. Who are you fighting? So not only did I not know who I was fighting, I had not told Jim or Brian Peters, who was promoting my Irish title fight. The first they would have known about was when they turned the tv on to see me fight live on Sky Sports. How bloody daft was I? As luck would have it, I got to the venue about 7pm and by 7.45 I was weighed in, had a medical and in the ring live on tv. It all turned out ok in the end, I won on points and walked away injury free. Brian and Jim were not happy the next day to say the least and they had every right to be. Brian shouted down the phone, "If anything had gone wrong the fight would have been off". It was a gamble but I made a few quid and the next day we went out and bought everything we needed for when the baby arrived.

The same day Brian sent over a contract for the Gomez fight. One of the stipulations was I could not take another fight before facing Gomez on January 28. Brian even called me to make sure I knew what I had signed. "Don't worry Brian," I said. "I won't push my luck again and I will see you at the press conference in Dublin in two weeks time".

Candice dropped me off at Gatwick Airport at 6am on the day of the press conference. I remember sitting in a coffee shop while I was

127

waiting for my flight to be called when the famous tv psychic Uri Geller walked past. Never one to miss an opportunity, I walked up to him, explained that I was fighting for the Irish title in a few weeks and would he wish me luck? Uri looked me straight in the eyes and said," you will not need any luck, you are going to win". He then said, where I was going. I said I'm off to Dublin for the press conference, the fight is in eight weeks' time. He asked where I was training and I told him I'm training in London; I'm only going to Dublin for the day. He said he was off to Dublin as well for a tv show and asked for my contact details. He gave me his contact details as well and said when you are back, give me a ring and we could meet up as he would like to come to the gym and watch me train.

Like most big fights the press conferences can get pretty lively and this one was no different. We were exchanging some pretty nasty insults when all of a sudden, Gomez jumps up, and flips the table in the air so I jumped up and we went head to head. Then Gomez stuck the nut on me. No sooner had he done that then former heavyweight big Joe Egan stepped between us and grabbed Gomez and pushed him away. "That's a fucking liberty to do that" Joe told Gomez. I said, "Don't worry Joe I'll even things up in eight weeks' time."

Big Joe was former world heavyweight champion Mike Tyson's sparring partner. Mike always called Joe the toughest white man on the planet. I was absolutely fuming after what Gomez had done to me. He never respected me at all. Even at the press conference he dismissed me and said he would take me out inside five rounds. Believe me, when I got home, I trained like a lunatic.

A week later I spoke to Uri and true to his word we arranged for him to come to the gym and watch me spar. Now this should have been a great time for me, training was going great, Uri was coming down to show some support and Candice and I were three months away from the birth of our first child. As I said earlier something always seems to happen to wipe the smile off my face.

Uri was due in the gym on the Tuesday but on the Monday evening Candice came home and was clearly upset and had been crying. "What's happened, is there a problem with the baby? "No, the baby's fine but there is a mole on my leg and the doctor thinks it may be cancerous," said Candice. "So, I need to have a small operation to remove it so the specialist can examine it to find out if it is or not."

I met Uri the next day and my head was all over the place. All I could think about was Candice. I really was an emotional and physical wreck. All my energy just seemed to drain from me over night. The last thing I could think about was fighting but Uri was great. He got me to focus and stay positive. It worked, I was worried sick about Candice and the baby but I also needed to stay strong.

A few days later Candice had the Mole removed and sent off to the specialists to find out if it was cancerous. In the meantime, I was traveling to Uri's house a couple of times a week so he could work on my mindset and maintain my focus on the biggest fight of my career. As well as all the training of course, I was still trying to support Candice as well, not only because of the operation but her hormones were all over the place as well.

Fight week soon came around and I was due to fly out to Dublin to face Gomez for the Irish lightweight title at the Dublin Stadium on January 28, 2006. I received a phone call on the Tuesday morning from Uri. He said, "I have spoken to my good friend Patrick Rocca (prominent Irish businessman) and he wants to fly you out to Dublin on his new 2006 Falcon private jet." I thought he was on a wind up but he just told me to meet him at Farnborough Airport at 8.30am on Tuesday morning. I could not believe what was happening. Not only was I realising a dream come true by fighting for the Irish title but I was flying there on a private jet. I had seen the small aircraft take off and land at Dublin airport since I was a boy and now, I'm the one landing on the tarmac and being fast tracked through customs like a VIP.

Candice and the rest of my team were flying out a couple of days later. It must have been very uncomfortable for Candice because not only was she awaiting the results of her cancer test but she was also eight months pregnant. So that was on my mind as well. At the press conference on the Thursday Gomez was getting very personal again, trying to wind me up but I sat silently throughout and let him carry on talking bollocks. I think I wound him up more by not biting and saying a word. As I said Gomez was a very good fighter, who had previously

129

been one of the main headline boxers on Sky Sports. At the weigh in the next day there was tv cameras everywhere and as you can imagine the sports media were all over Uri, wondering what a famous spoon bender was doing at a boxing weigh in. I remember looking down and on one of the chairs there was a leaflet from a betting company displaying the odds for my fight with Gomez. The cheeky bastards had me as 125-1 in every round. You wouldn't give a three-legged horse those odds in the bloody Grand National, would you? The weigh in was televised and I'm told about three million people tuned in to watch it. Not wishing to disappoint our public, the inevitable happened at the traditional head to head photo session when Gomez got vocal again and we ended rolling around on the floor. Again, Big Joe Egan had to separate us. 'Leave it until tomorrow night,' said Big Joe.

The hardest thing for me was, because we were both staying in the same hotel, there was security everywhere, 24/7. It was like being banged up in Belmarsh again. That evening Candice and me were in reception when Gomez and his team came in from outside. Gomez walked straight up to my face and shouted, "you're getting knocked spark out tomorrow." I would not have put up with that from anyone but it was worse because Candice was with me so really gave it back to him. "Your tough saying that in front of my eight-month pregnant girlfriend. I've had plenty of experience with bullies like you from a kid. It's not what you can give that counts it's what you can take. Tomorrow night there will be just you and me in the ring, let's see how tough you are then?

I heard rumour that after we had had words at reception Gomez had gone back to his room and smashed it up. I had got into his head. On the day of the fight everything I had visualised in my mind was coming true. Uri came into my room and asked how I was feeling. I told him I was ready to fulfil my dream and make my friends and family proud. When we got to the Dublin stadium the atmosphere was electric, it really was. Apparently, the stadium is the only stadium in the world which is purpose built for the sport of boxing. How true that is I do not know. There were newspapers everywhere with front page headlines like 'Gomez and McDonagh in weigh in bust up'. I had never seen so many cameras flashing. After picking up my gloves Uri, my manager Jim Evans, trainer George Woodman and his son, Jamie all crammed into my tiny changing room. It was like a bloody broom cupboard so

130

when the boxing inspector came in to inspect my gloves you could not put a fag paper between us. Once my bandages were wrapped, I had to go outside into the corridor to warm up and get a sweat on for the cameras.

A couple of minutes later I was summoned to make my way first, to the ring. It was a long corridor out to the arena and Gomez's changing room was at the end before the walk up the steps. I could see the door open and he was smashing the lockers with his gloved fists and saying, 'this is world class now'. He probably left the door open on purpose knowing I had to walk past so he could try and intimidate me. Just like the night before, that backfired as well because I shouted through the door, 'you are one ugly motherfucker,' before walking up the steps to my entrance music of The Fields of Athenry. Any boxer will tell you this. When you walk up to the ring in a packed arena to your own motivational song the hairs on the back of your neck stand up and a mixture of nervous excitement flush through you in preparation for battle.

Even the hostile chants of 'you're getting knocked in two rounds' was not enough to distract me. As long as Candice, Tish and my brothers were there that was all that mattered. As I walked up the three steps to the ring I said to Candice, 'watch this'. I then grabbed the top rope and jumped it; the crowd loved it. Then the whole place went quiet as an arch of Sombreros appeared. Gomez's real name was Michael Armstrong but because of his reputation for fighting like a Mexican he changed it to Gomez, hence the Sombreros. The crowd went wild as Gomez stood in the archway, lapping up the attention and feeding off the energy his fans were generating. Gomez eventually entered the ring and paraded up and down like a lion waiting to be unleashed. I just thought to myself, 'I'm gonna tame you. He tried everything in the book to intimidate me. My introduction took about 30 seconds, his took six minutes, and he had about six people around him parading all kinds of different belts including the British and WBU world crown. It was pretty obvious who the house fighter was and it was not me. I had been an underdog all my life so this was just another day in paradise for me. All I was interested in was that Irish lightweight belt.

At last, the referee called us to the centre of the ring after a little talking to the bell finally rang. Gomez came out like a man possessed, trying to catch me cold from the off. I just tucked up and when an opening came, I flicked out a few jabs to let him know I was not going to roll over. As I went back to my corner after the opener the commentator was going bonkers, raving about how much of a monster Gomez was. I did much the same in second round, tucked up, stuck out my jab and connected with a few right hands. As the ref pulled us apart to end the round I looked straight into his eyes and said, 'it's going to be a long night, I'm not going anywhere.'

I upped the pace in the third round by raining in some body shots and uppercuts to slow him down and that seemed to work. Just before the fourth round started, I turned round to my team in the corner to say 'he is getting tired' George asked how I was feeling and I said, 'I haven't even started yet'. I changed my tactic again in the fourth round by moving around more with my hands down and looking for sharp jabs to keep him off balance. I could see he was getting frustrated because he was looking for the big right hand. The more desperate he got the more wildly he swung and missed. After yet another wild attempt at a haymaker I slipped it and unloaded a right hand to split open his eyelid. Blood started pouring down his face. The caged animal was now a wounded one and as the bell rang for the end of the fourth, I could see the panic on the face of his trainer Billy Graham. When I got back to my corner George said, 'He's ready to go, he's a beaten man but do not do anything silly because he is a big puncher and a desperate fighter is a dangerous fighter.

I was off my stool even before the 10 second warning, I could not wait to get at him. It looked like the cut man Mick Williamson was making a career out of treating him because he was still in the ring after the bell rang. Gomez flew out of the corner like a wild man, just like he did in the opener. I tucked up again. I thought either he was getting his second wind and I could be bang in trouble or is he was just blowing his beans? By now the crowd were on their feet thinking Gomez has got me hurt. We are now a minute and half into the round and he pushes me back onto the ropes. I held him around the back of the elbow with my left hand to stop that arm working. I then put in two big right uppercuts, one to the body and the other to the face which sprang his head back violently with no reply. The referee broke us up. I heard someone shout from my corner, "I think he's done; he's emptied his tank. Pick up the pace Peter". Gomez came marching forward again but I went right through him and got through with a big right hand over the top and a left hook to the body. I heard the air leave his body and he turned his back on me. He looked as though he just gave up, just stopped boxing or defending himself but the referee never jumped in, so I kept punching until he hit the canvas with a big right hook. He got up and just started walking to his corner. I must have hit him with about eight punches without reply before referee Sean Russell called off the fight. It reminded me of when Roberto Duran turned his back on Sugar Ray Leonard in their famous 'No Mas' fight in 1980. Regardless of how the fight ended I had kept my promise to my family and achieved my dream of becoming champion of my country. But it was not just the fact that I had fulfilled my dream and promise of becoming champ. I had come from sitting in a prison cell not knowing where my future lay, drinking myself silly in Ireland for months on end, and worrying about Candice's health, to having that belt wrapped my waist. I just thought, 'no matter what else I achieve in my life it will not come close to topping this night.'

As soon as I got out of the ring, I was rushed from one interview to another when all I wanted to do was see Candice, spend time with my family, and celebrate. I also wanted to thank Uri Geller because he was a big part of my camp. He kept my mind on the job while I was worried sick about Candice. As soon as we got back to the changing room, I was drug tested and quickly taken to a room where a press conference was hastily arranged. Because of all the post fight excitement and various ringside interviews, I was unaware of what was to come. Gomez was nowhere to be seen which was strange, especially as the fight had ended so bizarrely. As soon as I sat down with my promoter Brian Peters and coach George Woodman there were cameras and flashes going off everywhere, then all of sudden a reporter shouted out, "Peter, you were a 125/1 underdog, how did you do that, did Gomez take a dive? I just could not believe it. There I was sitting there with two swollen eyes and ice packs on my face thinking this is the best day of my life, then someone just asked me if Gomez threw the fight and was I in on it? That was just the start of it because, I did not know at the time, but one of the boxing pundits in the RTE studio, Irish boxing legend

Steve Collins said live on tv that "I smell a RAT everywhere, he could not do that, I want an investigation into this"

I sat in that conference for 20 minutes with reporters firing questions at me from all angles with accusations of the fight being a fix. After a while I just blew my top and said, "look, do I look like a man who has been in a fixed fight? Look at the state of my eyes, I think I have broken a rib as well." I went from cloud nine in the changing room to the same man struggling with my mental health back in Ireland. I just got up and left and said I would not be talking to any more Irish media.

I went back to my hotel and just cried my eyes out. My family were celebrating in the bar but I just could not face it. I was really proud of what I had achieved. I had worked really hard to fulfil my dream against all the odds and personal trauma. Uri came up to the room and asked why I was not in the bar celebrating with my family. "Uri, they(media) think I cheated. They have robbed me of my glory". "Don't worry about it Peter," said Uri. You will go down in history, you have done it, any publicity is good publicity. I said, "are you joking? Uri replied, "you know you won fair and square and that will be in your heart forever, that's all that matters. Now come down and enjoy your win with your family."

I woke up the next day and went down to breakfast to find the national newspapers were pretty much leading with allegations of the fight being fixed and that an investigation was under way. Both mine and Gomez's purses were being withheld pending the outcome of the investigation. Boyle Sports, a well know betting shop had announced that they had lost a lot of money as a result of my win over Gomez. I was a proud Irish champion on home soil but all I wanted to do was go back home London. Uri told me to go back to Connemara with your sister and Candice, and enjoy being a champion.

I took his advice and flew back to Connemara. Even when I got to the airport I was mobbed by reporters. They were not interested in pictures with me and the belt, all they wanted to know was, did Gomez and me fix the fight? I just told them if this is how you treat your champions you can fuck off.

When we landed in Galway, I thought I was still going to get hassled by the media about alleged fight fixing. I need not have worried because although Dublin was 200 miles away, I may as well have been in a different country. As soon as the plane door opened, I was greeted with 'welcome home champ, we knew you could do it.' As we made our way along the Wild Atlantic Way coast line there was a bonfire every five miles as a sign of respect. They always do that in Connemara when an all Ireland title has been won. I felt like a proper hero. I had no money in my pocket because the Boxing Board had withheld my purse money because of the investigation. But I was full of pride and we stopped off at the same pub I was at five years previously when I promised my Godfather Porick that I would return as the Irish champion. The pub was packed and before I knew it, I had downed about 10 pints of Guinness. I made my way to the beer garden outside and there was an almighty cheer from lots more people. There were also reporters, cameras flashing, everyone was so happy. "I done it all for you and my family, I was never gonna lose that fight."

Then someone came over and said, "Peter, come over here, there is a very special person here that I would like you to meet." There are three small islands off the coast of Connemara called the Aran Islands and can only be accessed by boat or plane. I was led to a car where a little old lady was sitting. I know it is rude to ask a lady here age but she must have been at least 100 years old. As she reached out to shake my hand she said, "Peter, you have made the whole of Ireland proud. I watched you on RTE. I have never left the Aran Islands in my life but I told my son this is a very special moment for a man from Connemara, County Galway to bring the title here from Dublin and I must meet you and thank you." This was a really special and humbling moment for me, to think that a lady of that age thought it important enough to leave her island for the first time to come and meet someone she did not know.

Another special person I met that day was Porick, who was quick to remind me of our conversation a few years earlier. "You did not just talk the talk, you walked the walk as well," said Porick. "You said you would be a national champion and you were true to your word." Candice and I spent another week in Connemara with Tish as there were a lot of demand for interviews with local radio and tv. I also spent time visiting local boxing clubs and spending time with other family members. It was a bit of a whirlwind to be honest and it did take our mind off going back home to find out the results of Candice's tests for a cancerous mole.

When we eventually got back home to Epsom, we got a phone call from the hospital saying that they would like us to come in and see them. This was two weeks before our first baby was due so you can imagine how stressful our train journey was to St Georges Hospital in Tooting was going to be. We never said a word to one another either on the hour-long train ride or the 15-minute walk from the station. Honestly, this trip to the hospital felt longer and more painful than my entire 12-week training camp for the Gomez fight. I would take getting punched in the head for 12 rounds any day. Once we got to the hospital the specialist sat us down. I remember it like it was yesterday. The room was cold and dark, it one of those rooms with no windows and always made you feel depressed. The doctor could see we were worried but he said, "don't worry its good news, the mole on your leg is not cancerous it's just unusual but you will be fine. As the tears of joy ran down my face I looked up at Candice and she had her head in her hands. It was a very emotional time. The tear of happiness and relief meant we could now concentrate on the birth of our first child. I could not thank the NHS enough they had been fantastic from start to finish.

The journey home felt seemed far quicker I can tell you. We were laughing and joking, it was in complete contrast to the trip there. You may have guessed already by now but not much seems to go smoothly in the McDonagh family. Two weeks after the due date Candice was taken in to hospital to be induced and six and a half hours later a beautiful 7lbs 1oz baby girl was born. Shannon May McDonagh arrived at 2.36pm on 12th of May at Epsom Hospital in Surrey. I can honestly say it was the most amazing experience of my life. I will never forget holding her for the first time and watching those big eyes of hers open and looking around at the bright lights and everyone making a fuss of her. Becoming a father for the first time meant boxing had to take a back seat. All I wanted to do was be with my little girl and Candice. We were now a proper family.

The other good news was I finally got cleared of any fight fixing allegations and was paid in full without any stain on my professional or personal character. It took six weeks to clear me but at least my good name was intact. However, the problem I had now was, I was considered too dangerous for the champions to face in terms of risk and reward and also too much of a risk for the unbeaten prospects climbing up the rankings. That's boxing politics for you, maybe that's a boxing book for me to write in the future.

The reality was I never got paid for my next three fights. In fact, I had to pay the opponent. Can you believe it? I was a champion that never got paid but had to pay the opponent out of my own pocket. As I said I will leave the politics for another day. I must thank my sponsors, though. I will forever be grateful and must say a big thank you to Jackie and Les Ironman from Southbank Fresh Fish and the late Patrick Rocca. Without them I could not have continued to fight and concentrate on my boxing career. Nearly two years after defeating Gomez my sponsors faith in me was rewarded when I was nominated for a crack at European light welterweight champion Giuseppe Lauri in Milan, Italy on the 29 February, 2008.

My manager Jim Evans phoned and said, 'pack your bags you got a European title shot'. It was a weight above but it could have been at heavyweight for all I cared. I had been waiting for this shot for two years and I was going to take it. Lauri was an experienced operator, who had had twice as many fights as me and been in with the likes of Ricky Hatton and Junior Witter. And to make matters worse I was facing him in his own back yard. It was a long-standing joke in British boxing circle that if you fought an Italian in Italy you had to knock them out to get a draw. I soon found out how true that saying was.

Come fight night I was so proud to fly the Irish flag in the ring and listen to the National Anthem. I just thought my dad will be so proud and I could not wait to bring that title belt back and show him. To cut a long story short the fight was pretty even at the end of the fifth round but I had sustained nasty cut. I got back to the corner and asked the cut man how bad it was. He replied, 'Don't worry it's only a scratch'.

I went out in the next round and caught Lauri with a beautiful combination of punches that had him collapsing on the ropes. I honestly thought I had him. Suddenly the referee shouted, 'stop boxing.' I was then led to a neutral corner where the doctor was waiting to examine the cut around my eye. After some conversation in Italian the referee waved the fight off. I could not believe it. After the fight I went to my changing and the doctor came in to check me over. I said, "Is the cut bad, how many stitches do I need? He just looked at me and replied, "its fine, its ok now". So yes, the rumours about fighting in Italy are true in my opinion.

By now I was beginning to fully understand how boxing works. Unless you were a Ricky Hatton or a Tyson Fury it did not matter how good you were you were never going to earn fortunes. The top and bottom of it is, unless you are regularly on PPV you're going to have to get a job. I now had a young family to support so I had to fight at short notice. Half the time I was not asking what the money was. I was a fighter, that was my job so I just got on with it. The fighting inside the ring was easy the harder fights for me were on the streets. I could see myself a journeyman fighter, boxing up and down the country and overseas against local prospects but that was not me. I could have earned good money but I was a champion and as far as I was concerned that was not an option.

Chapter 26
Working in Canada.

When it was just Candice and me, I did not have to worry about money as much but now Shannon had arrived, and money was becoming tight. So, I sat down with Candice and said, "look, money and boxing are not regular or good enough, and I'm not getting the right opportunities". Truth of the matter was I was probably not disciplined enough, and I was starting to realise that boxing was becoming a self-harming tool. Instead of physically cutting or hurting myself Like a lot of people do, mine was more mentally harming myself by accepting pain from opponents.   Maybe my form of self-harming had all started at a young age when my mum first left us and then kept coming back. The way she treated us kids and my dad were absolutely heart breaking. I just accepted that type of pain as something that happened in everyday life so the more punches, I took the more I accepted it.

It is also fair to say that anyone that knows me will tell I do not do anything by halves. If I am going to do something it has to be one hundred percent. My mind races faster than a formula one car and a friend once told me that I could meet myself coming and going. I will give you an example. When I told Candice I was going to get a full time job, she said, "what are you going to do and where? I said "CANADA".

As you can imagine she looked at me and said, "that's hallway around the world, why Canada? "Because if I stay here, get a job and the phone rings for a fight I will take the fight so I need to get away from boxing for a while. I need to think about our little baby now and us going forward. A friend of mine has a company, Tarmacking the roads and its really good money.

"Even if I just go for a couple of months to see how it goes". I was used to being away in camps so it was not unusual for me to be away. Candice said, "when are you going? 'Monday", I replied. "Monday," said Candice. "It's Friday now." "I know, I need to pack. Shannon was still very young but Candice knew I was only trying to give us a better life as a family. I promised Candice I would come back every eight weeks.

I flew out on the Monday from Heathrow Airport. It was hard saying goodbye to Candice and seeing the little tears run down Shannon's face but I knew I had to do it. I could not wait to get to Canada and phone Candice to reassure her not to worry. The plan was to stay out there for eight weeks and come back but after three weeks I really started to struggle. I was missing Candice and Shannon and when I am struggling there is only one place for me to be and that is a boxing gym. Luckily for me there was a gym not far from my apartment in Toronto.

I took myself down there and started doing some work on the heavy bag and not long after the gym owner asked me if I wanted to spar. I did not need asking twice. It is like asking a kid in sweet shop if they wanted some sweets. I borrowed some gloves and a headguard and told them I had a gumshield. Of course, I never did have a gum shield otherwise they would not have let me spar. I did a good six rounds and felt like I was walking on air. As soon as I got back to the apartment, I rang Candice. She said, "you sound happy have you been out drinking? I said no, I have found a boxing gym. I made her laugh because she said, "You have been half way round the world to get away from boxing and you go and find a boxing club. If it makes you happy then I'm happy."

They say everything in life happens for a reason. The following day, Saturday, I was shopping in Toronto with my mate Charlie, who owned the company I was working for. He loved his shopping and was always buying new stuff. One of the many shops we went into was a place called New York Fur. I am not really into fur coats but one really stood out. It was a Mink 164 Bomber jacket. I asked the shop assistant how much it was and she replied $7,500. I was earning good money tarmacking roads but that was well out of my price range. I then overheard a conversation at the front of the shop and boxing was mentioned. From what I could make out the shop was sponsoring a professional boxing show at the Powerade Centre in Mississauga in two weeks' time. I said to the gentlemen, "sorry to interrupt your conversation but I hear you are sponsoring a boxing show and I would like to buy a ticket." The man replied, "I am promoting it, where are you from? I said was from Ireland, but I lived in London and was working out here for a few months. I told him I was a former Irish professional boxing champion. He said, "are you retired? "No, fighters never retire," I replied. "My last fight was at 10 stone.

The promoter laughed and said, "you must have got paid a lot of money because you don't look hungry to me, what are now 13 stone? If you were around 11 stone, I could have got you a fight. I've a got a boxer no one wants to fight. He has had nine fights and nine wins and nine knockouts." me being me I just could not help myself. I said, "I'll fight him, won't knock me out."

"The fights in two weeks' time, you won't make 11stone in two weeks," said the promoter. "You wanna bet I said? The worst thing anyone can say to me is that I cannot do something because I just have to prove them wrong.

I still had the Mink bomber jacket in the back of my mind so me being the cheeky so and so I am said, "I will be ready to fight in two weeks. If I beat your man, you pay me my purse and then you buy me the Mink Jacket? The owner turned to me and said, I will give you this jacket if you win." I told both of them they had a deal and took their contact numbers.

The two weeks quickly passed and after a combination of hard work on the roads all day and gym sessions in the evenings, I had lost the two stone and made the weight as promised. After weighing in I was asked what gloves I wanted. They honestly thought because he's a puncher it would be a walk over for him. I said, "give me the smallest gloves you have because he's not going to lay a glove on me. I will show you real boxing, hit and not be hit."

141

The lad I was boxing a Canadian based Romanian. He was tough but I gave him a boxing lesson. He was throwing some big bombs but missing wildly. I was showboating a bit and very nearly knocked him out in the last round. I won the fight clearly on points. He was the local favourite, and the crowd were pretty hostile towards me when I walked up to the ring but once the fight was over, I had won them over. In the changing room afterwards the owner of New York Fur shop came up to me and said that the Mink Bomber jacket would be waiting for me to pick up in the shop next week. Fair play to him, he said, "Well done, I never thought you would win that fight. I didn't even think you would lose the two stone."

I got paid twice so it was a good night's work. I never told Candice I was boxing because I did not want to worry her. It was not the first time I had taken a fight without her knowing. I was straight on the phone to her afterwards. I said, "guess what? She replied, "what have you done now? I told her I had boxed and won on points. There was a short pause for a moment, then she nervously said, "you are joking? Candice knows better than anyone how spontaneous and unpredictable I can be but even she could not believe I could travel halfway around the world and arrange a fight within a month of being in the country.

Chapter 27

A joyous occasion is married by heartache.

Three weeks later I flew back to London for Shannon's first birthday. I cannot describe how great it was to see them for the first time in months. I never intended to box again but boxing was my escape from the reality of everyday life, and as I said, became a sort of self harming. I continued to travel backwards and forwards to Canada and to take fights here and there. We were doing ok for money and life was on the up, so I decided to stay home for a while. Then Candice fell pregnant again and we welcomed our second daughter into the world, the beautiful Marni. Shannon was now four and our little family was now complete.

It really was a dream come true but as I said earlier as soon as something good happens and life is good, either someone or something happens set us back. The arrival of Marni was a truly joyous occasion but that joy did not last long because four months after Marni's birth Candice was diagnosed with the early stages of Cervical Cancer.

It was hard looking after our two beautiful girls, but we had to stay strong for them. Candice was trying to stay strong. I can only imagine what she was going through and I was breaking down crying my eyes, worried sick about her and the girls. I used to watch Candice from a distance, either playing or cuddling the girls and it would start me off. I felt so weak and vulnerable, there was just nothing I could physically do to make things right again.

Not long after diagnosis, we were referred to the Cancer specialist at Epsom Hospital. The doctor said that they were going to operate on her in a couple of weeks. I could not help myself, I just came straight out with it, "Doc, what is the worst thing that can happen if this operation does not work? He looked me straight in the eyes and replied, "she could die". I just could not stay strong anymore. I know this was the second time Candice was having to go through this horrible experience, but I just could not stay strong anymore. Heartache had followed me around from a very early age and I suppose this was just one knock back too many and I just burst out crying like a baby. For the first time I felt like I needed my mum, not that I had ever experienced any love from her.

It should have been me comforting her but I'm ashamed to say it was the other way around. I remember looking at her and thinking, 'you are the strongest and bravest person I have ever met'. She then whispered in my ear, "I will be ok, I'm not going anywhere. I have two babies to bring up." At the same time my mind was racing, thinking, 'no mum for the girls, just like me. I had no mum either, what am I going to do? I felt so guilty and selfish for even thinking it. But as soon as she said, 'I'm not going anywhere', I knew she meant it. Then the specialist turned to Candice and said, you will be ok, stay positive we have caught this early. I will make sure I remove more than I need to, to make sure all the cells are clear. I then felt comfortable and more confident Candice was going to be ok.

As soon as we got home, I got changed and went out for a run. I told Candice that I needed to fight again. It is the only thing that can get me through this. Thankfully, the operation two weeks later was a success. Further check-ups were also good news. But because the bad always seems to follow the good in my life we were always anxious when the follow up scan every three and six months came around. Then the scans became yearly until Candice had been clear for three years.

By now I was in and out of the gym, winning some fights, losing others. I was becoming a journeyman fighter without even realising it, the exact opposite to what I always promised myself. It was late 2012 and a month before Christmas. I got offered a fight against a very good fighter named Bradley Saunders. Bradley was a gifted amateur and I accepted the fight in Manchester. The fight was over eight rounds and to be honest I got well beat and felt every shot. I thought, 'I got two young kids at home, I'm not getting any younger, is it time to hang up my gloves? Candice was now healthy again. I can just get a job back as a Fishmonger and make good money. My job was always open with Les and Jackie. I said to Candice, boxing is a hard sport, I am going to go back cutting and gutting fish. I did not care for the early starts and the hours were long and made me very tired, but the money was good. One Saturday morning just as I'm about to gut a Tuna I got a phone call. I picked up the phone and there was a northern accent on the end of it. "Hi Peter, Bradley Saunders". I said, "you on a wind up? "No, its me Bradley," replied the caller. "Do you wanna come up and do some sparring with me? I said, "You punched my head in last time why would you want to spar with me? "you're a good fighter," he said. "I learned loads from you, and I know I can learn more". I said, "I'm working now, let me get back to you later? He said, "fine, ring me later." I had a think about it and decided I was not really interested. The phone was still ringing, and I was taking fights here and there at short notice. I was silly, really because I was killing myself to make weight, working long hours and hardly training.

Chapter 28
Bad news from Ireland

I was sitting at home one evening after a hard day's work at the fish market when the phone rang, it was my sister Tish, and she sounded really upset. She did not beat around the bush; Tish just came right out with it. "Pete, I've been to the hospital today and been told I have cancer". My heart just sank. Again, life was just returning to some kind of normality after Candice's cancer scare, and now I'm going through the same thing with Tish. I know it sounds selfish, but I just did not know how much more heart ache I could handle. And I just felt so helpless because Tish was in Connemara and I was hundreds of miles away in Epsom, Surrey. I said, "you will be ok", I could feel she was being brave. I had been there twice with Candice and was a patron for a charity called Niamh's next step. The charity was named after five year old Niamh, who passed away in May, 2012 after an 18 month battle with Neuroblastoma.

There was never any question that I would not go out there to be with her and I insisted on taking the next flight out, but Tish said no because she was having more tests next week and will no more then. I asked how Tom, her partner was and the kids, Harry (4), and Saoirse (3). The kids were very young so would not understand much but Tish said everyone was good and staying strong.

I put down the phone and Candice said, "are you ok, you look like you have just seen a ghost? I just got up out of the chair and said, "I have got to go out, I'll be back soon." I got in my car and drove from Epsom to Bermondsey to be alone with my childhood memories where me and Tish grew up. They were not all great memories as I'm sure you know from what you have read so far. In fact, I made my way to the very spot by the Thames overlooking Tower Bridge where my dad tried to take his own life all those years before. The spot I, Tish and Liam took a very young Martin in his pram. It was not a nice memory but this was the point where we all became so close as a family. At that point I just broke down and cried. I sat there on the wall dangling my feet over the edge and just needed that hour to collect my thoughts and let out every last tear from my eyes drain away.

Once I had pulled myself together, I made my way back home to Epsom. I walked through the door and Candice asked if I was ok. "Candice, Tish has breast cancer". She just cuddled me and said, "she will be ok, they can do amazing things nowadays".

I was on the phone every single day trying to keep up with what was going on. I just could not think straight. I even stopped going to work, I would just sit at home all day waiting for the phone to ring. Every time it rang, I thought it was Tish. She had started her Chemo and was responding well. I was fed up sitting all day waiting for news, so I said to Candice that I was over to visit her and cheer her up. I went and bought a full-blown Leprechaun outfit. I wore it on the plane going out and all way to Tish's house. She did have a smile on her face when she opened the door. Even though I announced my arrival by saying I was her lucky Leprechaun it was a good job I had full head on because I had tears running down my face. I remember Tish turning her back to walk into the living room and she just looked so frail, half the woman I was used to seeing, it really did break my heart. I took the mask off to wipe my eyes when she was not looking. I stayed for a few days to help with Tom and the kids, they seemed to be coping ok.

When I landed back in England, Candice said that my trainer Ash had been trying to contact me. By now I had had more trainers than JD Sports. He said Bradley Saunders had been in touch about some sparring I thought I had better call him. I rang him and said that I have a lot going on at the moment and was sorry but had to refuse his offer. Bradley said, "Pete I'm in Spain in training camp. I will pay for you to come out, pay for all your accommodation, food and pay you wages for sparring. It will give you a bit of Christmas money".

Candice had overheard the conversation and told me to go because it would be good for me and take my mind off things. And if I did not like it, I could come home. I decided to take Bradley up on the offer and took a flight out the next day. I arrived in Marbella, Spain and headed straight down to the MGM Gym. I was still calling Tish every day for updates and Candice as well. The only time I was not thinking about them was when I was actually sparring. The MGM really was a lovely gym. I had travelled the world as a sparring partner. I had stayed pretty much everywhere on my travels from five-star hotels to caravans and Hostels, the best and the worst. But this was like a different world. Normally when you are hired as a sparring partner it is usually 'be here at this time, there at that time'. I never even knew how many rounds I was doing but at the MGM everyone was so friendly. Everyday someone would ask if everything was ok, how you are feeling. It was just a different world. I never once felt used. I even had someone in my corner giving me water and putting vaseline on my face. They were even shouting words of encouragement.

I was coming to the last week of sparring. I noticed one particular person come to the gym every day. He never said much but watched everything. Before I was getting ready to leave, he came up and gave me some water and said, "Peter, I watched a lot of your fights, you can really fight, why is your record so bad? I just told him that I never really been looked after, never really had time to properly prepare for fights. To be fair that was not entirely true because I had to take some of the blame as well for keep taking fights at short notice and not being disciplined enough to prepare properly.

I then completed my last spar and boxed really well, everyone clapped and cheered in appreciation at the end. Just before I was about to leave and catch my flight home, I thanked everyone for looking after me and then Bradley shouted over, "Peter, Daniel would like to see you before you go." Daniel was the one that was in the gym every day, not saying much but watching everything. He said, "When are you fighting again? I said that I did not know because my sister has cancer and I have a young family in England. And to be honest I did not know if I was ever going to fight again. He gave me his number and said that if I ever wanted to talk and you are struggling a bit give me a call. I said, "thank you, that means a lot" He must have seen that I was struggling with everything that was going on back home and maybe sensed that the only time I could forget about my sister was when I was in a boxing ring getting my head punched in

I flew back to London and stayed in contact with Daniel. He was on the phone daily, asking how I was coping and about my sister's health. A few months later I got a call from Tish. She sounded so excited. I said, "have you got some news? She then blurted out, "I've got the all clear". You have no idea how happy that news made me feel. It was like all my Christmas's had come at once. I think it was December 3 ,2003. I was ringing around everyone to give them the good news.

I spoke to Daniel; he was buzzing for me, and again my emotions were all over the place. He said I was welcome out to Marbella any time to train and help me get back to winning fights again. I made it clear I was not interested I just wanted an easy life. I had my family, and my sister back with the all clear, and I was just going to enjoy Christmas. I did not care if I was stacking shelve or cleaning out toilets, I had had enough of fighting, inside and outside the ring.

Daniel said. "I don't care whether you box again or not, I'm your friend and am here for you, you're a great person". Christmas was close and I had just celebrated my 36th birthday on December 21. I was out with the lads and a bit worse for wear after downing more than a few pints of Guinness when the phone rang. It was my Aunt Margaret. She was a very religious person, who used to carry around the Padre Pio glove. Padre Pio was the Saint Pius of Petrolina. The glove was a very holy garment and she used to travel the world healing people with it.

In a broad Galway accent, Margaret said, "Pete, Tish is back in hospital and she's not good". I replied, "please don't tell me the Cancer is back? She said, "yes, there's no rush but you better comer over and see her." "I'm booking a flight right away," I said. As it was the holidays it was very difficult to get a flight. The only one I could get was January 3. I then got another call from Margaret on December 30 saying, "you had better get over here as fast as you can, Tish has been put in a hospice and she may not make it through the night. She in terrible pain and the doctors are pumping her full of morphine".

Aunt Margaret had been around sick people all her life and she knew when a person's life was coming to an end. She said the priest was coming at 8pm. It was now 10am in the morning. I told her. "I'm going to call Liam and Martin. We will get there somehow. Tell Tish we are on our way."

That same day I got text through from Daniel in Spain, wishing me and my family a Happy New Year. I rang him straight away to tell him Tish was in a Hospice and that I got to get Ireland as quick as possible. I explained that I was trying to get a flight to Ireland but so close to New Year it was becoming impossible. Daniel said, "leave it to me, get your bags packed. Is Candice going? I said, "no just me Liam and Martin."

He told me to "text through their name's and I will would get the flights sorted. Just worry about getting to the airport". I told Liam and Martin
150

to pack a bag because we are going today, the flights were getting sorted now. True to his word, Daniel phoned and said, "you're flying out at 1.50pm from Gatwick to Dublin. There will be a car waiting for you to take you to the Galway Hospice, you will be there by early evening."

We got to the Hospice around 6pm. I will never forget that day. It was a dark, cold and stormy night. We all rushed in to the reception and quickly asked where Tish's room was. When we got there the rest of the family had already arrived. Liam and Martin lagged behind me and were really struggling to come to terms seeing Tish the way she was. Neither one of them had mentioned a single word on the plane or in the car on the way to the Hospice. You have to remember that Tish was like a mum to us three boys, even when mum was there, but even more so when she left. So, to see this lovely, strong and feisty lady a complete shell of herself, was incredibly heart breaking. I too was struggling badly but I wanted to stay strong for Liam and Martin.

As I held her hand my nephew said, "Pete, she has not opened her eyes for hours". As he said that, Tish opened her eyes, smiled and said, "what are you doing here? I kissed her on the head and said, "I have come to see you." Liam and Martin were standing behind me with their heads bowed down. They both muttered quietly, "are you ok? Then they both left the room. Martin was the baby and Liam and Tish were like twins growing up, and like I said they were struggling big time. Up to this point in my life I had been through a lot, and I was tired and exhausted but I knew I had to be strong for my brothers and the rest of the family.

The priest came in around 8pm to read Tish her last rights. That's when it really hit me, the realisation that I was going to lose my lovely sister. The Priest usually reads the last rights just before someone passes away. I told him that she was not ready to go yet but aunt Margaret said, "Pete, let the Priest do his job, god forbid we lose her." So, the Priest said a prayer and so did my aunt. I stayed in that room all night with her. She was in terrible pain and would scream out. I would get the nurse and they would give her more morphine.

When the sun came up, Tish was still with us and seemed to be perking up a bit. She had her eyes open and was asking questions. It was now New Year Eve, 2013 and all the family were gathered around her bed. My dad was still in England. They were very close, and he just could not face seeing Tish laying in a hospital bed and suffering like this. We rang him and put him on the phone to her. Speaking to dad really made her smile. Tish was still fighting hard to stay awake and engage with us but equally she fell into uncontrolled unconsciousness. The pain she was suffering was now getting worse by the day and by January 3 Liam and Martin just could not take seeing her suffer any further and announced they were going to get the next flight home. They were staying in the hotel down the road, and they did insist that I had a few hours away to gather my thoughts but I was not going to leave until she passed away. Before Liam and Martin went, I whispered in their ears, that 'she would be gone soon so say your good byes now.' They both cuddled and kissed her, and said how much they loved her. Martin left in floods of tears but not before saying, "Thank you so much for being a mum to us". Listening to what Martin had said broke my heart.

Once everyone had gone, I laid on the bed with Tish and she turned to me and said, "Pete, why is everyone crying? I told her it was because "they could see that you're not well." "I'm so scared, Pete, I just want to go home." Tish was repeating this every day that she was in the hospice until she could not speak anymore. "I'm going to die and leave my babies and my two brothers." I just kept repeating, "please don't be scared Tish, the kids will be fine, we will look after them and make you proud."

This was probably one of the hardest conversations I have ever had with anybody and was ever likely to have. Holding back the tears as best I could I told Tish, "I'm going back to boxing again, this will break me if I do not focus on boxing again. I'm lying here seeing what a fighter you are. We are the fighting McDonagh's, and I want you to you proud." Even though she was so weak, Tish did manage to cuddle me, and I felt her energy. She then said, "promise me, if you fight again, promise me you will never lose again?

With tears running down her face I can honestly say I felt the energy leave her body and transfer into mine. I felt so strong. I said to her, "Tish, I will never lose again, I promise you."

My record at that time was 20 wins and 28 losses, I was 36 years old and definitely in the twilight of my career, as they say. Unless you're a heavyweight, fighters are usually past their prime in their late twenties or early thirties. The next day I just felt so strong and full of energy whilst Tish by now drifting in and out of a coma. She described the pain as like snakes squeezing her so tight, she could not breath. I was going crazy seeing her suffer. At one point I went into the chapel at the Hospice and prayed. I said, 'if there was really a god, please take my sister now, don't let her keep suffering like this?

The doctors could only give her so much morphine, but I really was at the end of my tether. I could not see her go through any more pain, to the point that I had thoughts about smothering her by putting a pillow over her face and putting her out of her misery.

The suffering went on until January 5. I called her son Harry and her partner, Tom into the room. We were all sitting around the bed, and I told her our dad was here. She was in and out of consciousness by now, and pretty much totally unresponsive. I said, "dad's here now, but he doesn't want to talk, he's too upset". I told her he was holding her hand. At this point there was no movement. I told Tish, dad wanted to play a song for her. With that I played the song Daddy's Girl on my phone. As it was playing, tears ran down my cheeks and I whispered gently in her ear, 'You can go to sleep now Tish. A beaming smile lit up

153

the room but soon after her hand became limp and dropped down by the side of the bed. She then started breathing heavily through the nose as her airways became permanently blocked. Harry was next to me, and her partner Tom was on the other side of the bed. Tom and Tish rarely saw eye to eye, but I linked their hands and said you got to be strong for each other. I said my goodbyes to Tish and told her I loved her and would see her on the other side. "This is your time now to say goodbye", I told Tom and Harry. As I walked outside I took one last look at my lovely sister knowing full well I was never going to see her again. After 10 minutes of me sitting outside gathering my thoughts, Tom came out of the room and said, "She gone".

Harry was still in the room cuddling his mum. It was heart breaking to see. In Ireland it is our custom to stay with the deceased until the morning, when the funeral directors come in, take the body and prepare them for the funeral. I will never forget it. From 1.45am when Tish was officially pronounced dead on January 5 until 9am we sat with her. That seven hours soon passed very quickly as we shared all our fond memories and celebrated her life. Tom and Harry did say that one of Tish's wishes was to have all of us wearing matching suits to wear. She even travelled to Galway a few months earlier to arrange and pay for the suits. Right up to the end our Tish was still looking out for all of us. It is an Irish custom for a funeral to take place three days after a death. We also have a two-day wake followed by the funeral on the third day. After leaving the hospital, myself Tom and Harry got in the car and immediately made our way to Carraroe. As soon as Tom started the engine Michael Buble's song, I wanna go home started blurring out on the radio. "That's exactly what Tish kept saying when I first went to see her in the hospice," I said. I knew then that Tish would be with us forever, which made her passing much easier for me to accept.

I remember driving along the Wild West Atlantic coastal road towards Carraroe very clearly. It was a bright day, and the sun was breaking through the clouds over the Galway Bay. We stopped off at the pub for a pint of Guinness before picking up Tish's coffin. Then, Tom and Harry dropped me off at the graveyard overlooking the sea. I went there to dig

Tish's grave. The plot is situated in one of the most beautiful, picturesque and most peaceful places in the world, in my opinion. My grandparents and my uncle were also laid to rest there.

As I was about to start digging, my cousin Marcus arrived and said, "Pete, are you sure you want to be doing this, are you ok? I will watch and if you need me, I'm here". The beach overlooking the graveyard was the same one my dad used to pick Winkles from to make a bit of extra money when I was a kid, and the same place my life flashed before me as a six year-old when I got stranded on my favourite Rock.

"Pete, I'm gonna take the lorry down the Dolin and get some fresh Coral sand to go on top of the grave," said Marcus I was so focused on digging Tish's final resting place that I was totally oblivious to people coming up to offer their condolences. I was not being rude I was just so fixated on the job that needed to be done. Then all of a sudden, the heavens opened up. Believe me, when it rains in Connemara, it absolutely buckets down. As quick as I was digging out the soil, the water was filling up the hole even quicker. I remember looking up at the Sky with the rain and tears running down my face and just collapsing in the hole. It suddenly dawned on me that Tish was dead, and at that moment I finally started grieving. When Marcus came back he found me nearly six foot down in the grave, up to my waist in water and crying my eyes out. Marcus dragged me out, took the shovel off me and said, "Leave the rest to me, I'm gonna finish this off". I replied, "no you're not", and took back the shovel and dug down a few more feet, then Marcus, said, "Ok Pete, that's enough, level up the ground and that will be ready for Tish."

I had not slept for days so I went back to Tish's house to get my head down for a couple of hours. Not long after, Liam and Martin knocked on the door and asked when we were going to dig Tish's grave. I told them I had already dug it. "You dug it on your own? said Liam. "Yes", I replied, "come on, you and Martin can buy me a pint down the local village pub". The pub was already packed when we got there. As I said earlier It is traditional to have a three-day wake but I only stayed for a short time because I had a lot to do the following day to make sure Tish had a great send off. Tish was laid out in an open coffin in the funeral house. I am not joking, the entire village and the surrounding villages as well, came to pay their respects. From 12pm until 6pm there were people in and out nonstop for six hours, no gaps at all. I was so touched to see how many people had turned out. She was only 43 but was an influence on so many people's lives. So many people came to Connemara that day that the Garda spent hours re-directing traffic in the village.

It was a very sad day for the family and what made it worse for me was Tish's daughter Saoirse never left my arms throughout the entire ceremony. She was only five years old, and I had to be strong for her. Saoirse pointed to the coffin and said, "Is mummy in there?. I said, "yes" and she asked if she could give her mum a picture. How I kept myself together at that moment I really to this day do not know.

After the ceremony was completed, we drove Tish to her final resting place. Myself, Liam, Martin, Tom, Harry, and some cousins carried Tish onto the sand, across the beach and into the graveyard. Carrying that coffin across the sand was as tough physically as it was mentally. By the time we had got to the graveside we looked like we had just played 90 minutes of football. Our shoes and trousers were caked in mud, but we did not care. The priest conducted a lovely service at the graveside and when it was over myself, Liam, Martin and Harry all picked up a shovel each and started filling in the grave. Afterwards we added Coral sand on top to make the grave look clean and tidy. I like to think that we really did Tish proud that day. We all sat down and told our favourite stories about our lovely sister. Martin always loved telling people that Tish was his mum when she picked him up from school. Harry then told us she would tell stories about us all. She was so proud of us boys, and she knew we were equally as proud of her.

I really tried to keep it together for the sake of the family and be as positive as I could but the truth was, I was at the lowest point in my life. When I got back to England I was really struggling and out every day drinking. I just did not know where to turn. Thinking about it know I think I had spent so much time trying to stay strong and positive for everyone else that my mental health was steadily becoming increasingly worse by the day, and drinking was my release from facing up to the reality of everyday life. By now Candice could see how the drink was getting a hold over me, and she knows and understands me better than anyone. "I know its hard for you Peter. You have had a lot to deal with a lot over the years, but you do have a family here to look after." I had heard those words from Tish all those years ago back in Ireland and knew she was right. Candice also said that, 'Tish would not want to see you like this'. And she was right again.

Chapter 29

Another fight outside the ring.

Unless someone has suffered with mental health issues it is very hard to explain. But one thing is for sure, drink is never the answer. It just makes you feel more and more depressed and down. Boxing was always my coping mechanism when I felt so low. As much as boxing was a form of self harming for me it was also my saviour, something to focus on and forget about whatever horrible thoughts were living rent free in my head at the time. As has often happened in my crazy and unpredictable life, just when I'm slipping into my darkest mood a golden opportunity suddenly appears and snaps me out of it.

About 10 minutes after having the conversation with Candice the phone rang, it was Daniel, ringing from Spain to ask how I was coping after putting Tish to rest. "To be honest Daniel, I'm not in a good place. I'm out every day drinking, feeling sorry for myself and even getting angry with my friends". "Right, I'm gonna book you a flight tomorrow," replied Daniel. "Come out and see me, bring the family if you want to". After I got off the phone, I sat down with Candice and told her that I told Daniel how low I was feeling and he invited me over to Spain for a chat and a bit of a holiday. I also told Candice if I do fight again, I had promised Tish on her deathbed that I would never lose again and that I would win more titles. Tish had made me promise never to lose again but if I did there would be no more boxing for me.

Candice said, "And if you do lose again do you promise to keep your word? "yes", I said, "that's it for me, I mean it".

I flew to Marbella in southern Spain the next day to meet Daniel. I think it was around January 14. Daniel said, "I've seen a lot of your fights, and you can really fight you just don't seem to take it seriously? I told Daniel, "The only fight I ever took seriously was the Michael Gomez fight. Pretty much every other fight I had a couple of weeks notice. I'll be honest, since the Gomez fight, I think boxing just helped me get through life's battles and to exercise whatever demons were flying about in my head.

"I got on the plane today because, again at this time of my life I need boxing. It's the pill that takes the pain away". My eyes then filled up as I was talking and Daniel must have seen this because he grabbed hold of me, cuddled me and said, "I will look after you. If you want to fight again." I shook his hand and replied, "Here's my hand, this is my bond, if I lose again, its over. I promised my sister and I promised Candice".

"I take your word, no contract needed", replied to Daniel. "When do you want to fight again? I told him I would like to fight as soon as possible because it's my sister's birthday on March 17, St Patricks Day. "That's only eight weeks away," said Daniel.

"I know, I've taken fights at four hours notice live on Sky Sports, having eight weeks to prepare is a luxury for me," I said.

"That's all about to change for you now, "insisted Daniel. "You will get proper training camps. We will bring sparring partners, you will eat right, you will not be used anymore, and we will get you a sponsor".

I went home with my head a lot clearer. I told Candice what Daniel had said and that I was going to give boxing one last go and was going to do it right. I had been a professional for 10 years and always felt used and abused and that's the top and bottom of it. Daniel said he wanted to look after me, and what did I have to lose? I never had much to offer as I was on the scrap heap and taking fights here and there and not really taking boxing seriously. But when I shook Daniel's hand, I made a commitment and my honesty and loyalty was there. I also had a desire to make my sister and family proud and that was all the drive I needed.

A week later the phone rang and it was Daniel, calling to make the travel arrangements. "How will your family be coping with you over here for six weeks," said Daniel. "I have been all over the world as a sparring partner for the last 10 years, I will speak to Candice and get back to you as soon as possible." Before I could put the phone down Daniel said he had some good news. "I've got you a fight on the 15th," he said. "Of February", I replied back. "No, March 15." "But that's St Patricks weekend." "I know," said Daniel. "And is for the title, live on Channel 5 tv and its taking place in Reading." That was all I needed to know; I'll be there tomorrow."

When I told Candice she was over the moon for me. She was just happy I was happy. She did not like me fighting but I was already doing it before I met her, so she supported me all the way and was my biggest fan. As too was my girls, Shannon and Marni.

It was late January when my plane touched down and I arrived at the MGM Gym (later changed to MTK) in Marbella. It was a bit surreal because it was the middle of Winter but the heat hit me as soon as I got off the plane. The other funny thing was landing at Malaga Airport and driving along the coastal road to Marbella. The road ran parallel with the sea coast and reminded me of the trip from Galway to Connemara. Being so close to the sea brought back some emotional memories and made me feel closer to home, and Tish.

There weeks into my training things were going really well. I was getting so fit running up and down the mountains and training out in the open air. Daniel was by my side every day making sure everything was going the right way. He was not a boxer, but he loved the sport and did not like the way some fighters were being treated. I remember one particular day; it was a Monday and I was due to spar. The sparring partner was due to arrive from another part of Spain but for some reason or another he was unable to make it. I went ballistic when I found out. One thing I cannot do is hold my emotions too well and I tend to say what I feel. I do not mean everything I say but I just have to get it out of my system. Daniel must have heard me ranting and raving and came out of the office to see what was going on. "Pete, whats up you mad man? said Daniel. "My fucking sparring partner's not coming, my trainer's just got off the phone and confirmed it.

"Calm down," said Daniel. "I will go and get my gear on and spar you." "Are you having a laugh," I said. "I'll punch your head in." Daniel just laughed and said, "I'll be back in a minute." Five minutes later Daniel came back complete with gumshield, gloves and headguard. "I was still bandaging my hands but watched him shape up out the corner of my eye and thought, 'he looks like he knows what he's doing.'

I got in the ring, we touched gloves and then Daniel threw a lazy jab and a big right hand over the top that caught me bang on the chin. I'll be honest that punch shook me to my boots, I did not know if I was in London or Spain. That punch woke me up I can tell you. We ended up going six rounds and by the end his eyes were marked up and he had blood pissing out of his nose. I said, "Thanks so much, that session really helped me out." Daniel said, "I'll see you tomorrow." I said, "are

161

you serious? He said, "yes." Daniel ended up being my main and only sparring partner for that Irish title fight and he pushed me really hard in every session.

I flew back to London two days before the fight against John Hutchinson for the vacant Irish light middleweight title. Thanks to Daniel, I was fully prepared, the camp was great, and I knew I was going into this title fight in the best possible shape. The fight was live on Channel 5 in the UK, and I walked to the ring dressed up as an Irish Leprechaun, the crowd were in fits of laughter. It was a good job I had a mask on because I was crying my eyes out. Emotions were running high inside the protection of that mask because all I could think about was the promise I made to Tish on her deathbed and winning another Irish title so I could put the belt on her grave. I need not have worried, I comfortably out-pointed Hutchinson over 10 rounds and dedicated the win to her.

In the post fight interview I thanked Daniel for helping me prepare for the fight, the MGM Gym Marbella, I was proud to become their first champion. Being my sister Tish's birthday and St Patricks weekend just made everything perfect. The next day I flew back to Marbella to thank everybody in the gym, my manager, sponsors, that helped me prepare. The people there threw a big party to celebrate my win, and also I think to take my mind of Tish's birthday.

Over the next year I was backwards and forwards from Spain for training camps and won another couple no title fights. I was in a great place. Mentally, life was going really well then, I got an offer to fight Dean Byrne for the vacant Irish welterweight title. The thought of becoming a three weight Irish champion was far too good to refuse.

It was a bit of a grudge match because before the fight announced I was doing a bit of punditry work on Box Nation, you know, breaking down fights, etc. I was working with John Rawling, who is a real legend as a boxing commentator in my opinion. Even before the fight was announced with Byrne, there was a bit of needle between us. Dean was a top fighter, he had regularly worked as a sparring partner for world champion boxers Manny Pacquiao and Amir Khan at Freddie Roache's gym in Los Angeles, so he definitely knew his way around a boxing ring. Working on Box Nation was the perfect platform to sell the fight, especially as the fight was going live on that platform. The banter came to a head one day when Byrne called me a plastic paddy. I never said another word after that, just flew back to Spain, got my head down and prepared like never before. Dean was the favourite with the bookmakers. I had been the underdog pretty much all my life until Daniel came along so I was used to it. I really upped my training for this fight. Instead of running six miles a day I was running 10 and instead of doing 8x800 on the track I was running 12. I mentioned earlier that I had promised Tish I was not going to lose again and that was on my mind every day, right up to the day of the fight. I know I was putting unnecessary pressure on myself, but I needed that pressure to keep me motivated and disciplined.

The fight took place at the National Stadium in Dublin on November 7, 2015, just a month before my 38th birthday. Without going into too much detail I thought I boxed the best fight of my career to out-point Dean Byrne over 10 rounds. It just goes to show that if you put the work in it will pay off. I became a three weight Irish champion that night and I hope I did my family proud. I had been away at camp for eight weeks and it was great to see Candice and Shannon and Marni again. The girls were even interviewed on tv with me after. They are not shy in front of the tv cameras that's for sure. I did say after the fight that I wanted to bring the big fights back to the Dublin National stadium. I was buzzing, at the least I wanted a European title shot. But for now, I just wanted to spend time with my family and enjoy Christmas. I think it was around December 5, a month after the Dean Byrne fight, that the phone rang, it was Daniel. "Time to get back into training camp," said Daniel. "You're fighting in February. we are still trying to finalise a big fight."

To be honest I could do with a rest but I was not getting any younger so flew out to Marbella to start pre training. I had still been running at

163

home a couple of times a week to tick over but two weeks into camp in Marbella I injured my right shoulder. I went see the physio the same day and he told me to rest up for six weeks. "You have overdone it in training in back to back camps and at 38 year-old you need more rest." He spoke.

When I got back to the gym I told my trainer and Daniel what the doctor had said, that I need to rest up for six weeks. "I'll be ok, though", I said, "I have fought before like this, just let me fight? Daniel replied, " don't be stupid, that's why your record is the way it is and been beat by fighters that cannot lace you boots."

I was gutted at missing out on a big fight, especially as I was in the best form of my career but at least I could spend Christmas at home with Candice and the girls. I may not have been on the February 6 card in Dublin, but I was offered the next best thing when I got a call from Jim Bentley, from the production team at Box Nation. "Hi Peter, Its Jim. How do you fancy working on the February 6 card in Dublin?

"Of course,", I said, "yes". It is the next best seat in the house if you're not fighting. Jim made all the arrangements and I was on my way back to Dublin, but yet again I was caught up in tragedy but this time it was more devastating than I could possibly have imagined.

Chapter 30
Regency attack

Candice dropped me off at Gatwick airport at 6am on February 5. The airport was only a 30-minute drive from home and the flight to Dublin only took an hour, so I arrived at the Regency Hotel in plenty of time for the afternoon weigh in. All the fighters, officials and tv crews were staying at the Regency so it made sense for the weigh in to take place there. I had a quick coffee when I arrived then went up to my room to get a couple of hours sleep and a shower. I put on an MGM tracksuit and made my way down to the bar about an hour earlier than the weigh in to meet with the production team to discuss timings and schedules for the show the next evening. Once we were all briefed and were happy with everything I made my way to the big conference room where the weigh in was to take place.

The place was really buzzing with boxers, officials, families, fans, young and old. I was gutted that I was not fighting. I few of the lads on the show came up to me, telling me not to worry and that I will be on the next show. People were also saying what a great performance I put up against Dean Byrne and that I had to build on it.

When I saw Daniel, he told me he had a slot on the card, and did I want to fight? "of course, I do, yes," was my prompt reply. "Your mad you are," he said, "I was only joking. Don't worry I'm working on a big fight for you." I told him I was fully rested now so I want a date and to get back to Marbella to prepare. "Let's get tomorrow out of the way and we can sit down on Sunday and work out your next move? said Daniel.

All the while we were talking people were coming up and talking to me, wanting pictures and talking about the show. I really felt as though I was at the top of my game now and really looking forward to securing a career defining fight. When I'm working with tv as a pundit I always like to be at the weigh in because I like to see what shape the boxers are in and what their body language in like. It's like doing homework for the job the following day.

Eventually the announcer from the Boxing Union of Ireland picked up the microphone and announced that the weigh in for the Box Nation televised event from the National Stadium in Dublin, was about to start.

As the undercard boxers were called up the noise in the hall was becoming more and more deafening as some of the local boxers were announced. As well all the boxing officials and trainers, etc there were young kids and families there to cheer on the boxers. I looked around and thought, 'wow this atmosphere is incredible. If I was boxing Marni and Shannon would be here making the biggest noise of all'.

Next on the scale was highly decorated amateur Gary Sweeney, who was from my neck of the woods in Connemara, County Galway. Gary got on the scale wearing just a pair of pants with the Superman logo on them. At this point I was standing near the back of the room in front of some double doors to my right. As Gary was on the scale all the fans were clapping and cheering but all of a sudden everything seemed to pause to a standstill. Out the corner of my eye I could see an old man with a flat cap on and beside him was a man dressed as a woman and their arms were linked together. As the old man and the 'woman' walked past me they looked straight at me and a group of people.

166

Then everything seemed to speed up again, but it still felt as though we were in slow motion mode. I honestly do not know what made me look out of the corner of my eye because no one else seemed to notice. As Gary was on the scale, I said to the person standing next to me, "what the fucks going on here? He said, 'it doesn't look right.' As he said that the old man and 'woman' were about five metres in front of us, with their backs to us. The one with the flat cap put his arm behind his back and looked like he was struggling to get something out then all of a sudden produced a handgun and spun around. It was just like the movies but it was real, is the only way I can describe it. Even though he had struggled to get the gun out everything just seemed to be moving slowly. All of a sudden, he was face to face with us and people were screaming, 'he's got a gun.'

There was mayhem everywhere now and kids were screaming. For a split second I honestly thought I was a dead man. Then there was a bang as he shot into the ceiling. Everyone hit the floor. I looked around to see the double doors and thought, 'I'm out of here.' A few of the group I was with followed but everyone else hit the floor. I ran out of the doors into the corridor and through to the reception area. I thought do I run out of the front of the hotel or through another part of the hotel? As I was running, I saw two people running into the reception from the main entrance, dressed in black with what looked like machine guns. I carried on running but all I heard was 'bang, bang, bang' and it was not from a hand gun.

After what seemed like ages, I found a cupboard to hide in, and quickly threw myself in it. I was like a tiny cleaning store cupboard. Someone else had the same idea because before I knew it the door flung open, and they landed on my lap. The cupboard was under a set of stairs and we could hear people running up and down. We did not know what was happening but could still hear the gun shots from a distance. It was as if the hotel was under attack. I honestly do not know how long we were in that cupboard for, but it seemed like hours. All of a sudden everything went quiet. So quiet in fact you could hear a pin drop. As I stuck my head out of the cupboard door, I saw my friend and former fighter Tommy Martin.

As quietly as I could I grabbed Tommy's attention. He looked round and laughed before saying, "what you doing in there, are you ok? I told him there were people running around with guns shooting up the place. He just looked puzzled and replied," Shut up what you on about? I said, "Where have you just come from? He said he was sitting up in his room so never heard or saw anything. As we walked out to reception people were crying, everywhere we looked. By now Tommy had realised the seriousness of the situation and said," What the fucks happened here?

I looked across the reception area and saw someone laying on the floor. He lay totally still and blood was pouring from his head. I thought, 'I hope that's not David.' I was only talking to him moments before I saw the hand gun get pulled out from the old man's back pocket. David was telling me how much he enjoyed my fight with Dean Byrne a few months before. I put my head down and thought, 'please do not be dead?

By now I was in deep shock at what had just happened. I walked out of the reception and onto the steps outside the building. I shouted at the top of my voice, 'where are the ambulances, where the fuck are the ambulances? As mayhem was erupting all around me the Garda turned up. They walked up the steps and said, "What's been going on here? Someone then shouted out, 'get in there you dogs, people have been shot.'

These were crazy scenes because if this was England or anywhere else in Europe the hotel would have been surrounded immediately by the police with guns and cordoned off. I was completely numb at this point, thinking, 'is this a normal occurrence in Dublin'. I thought that London was like the wild west at times but this was on a different level. The police rushed in with the paramedics quickly behind them. They went straight to the body in the reception area. One paramedic dropped to her knee then got up and said to her colleague, 'He is dead, shot in the head'. They then ran into another part pf the hotel to look for other victims that may have been shot. By now the Gardai were everywhere and surrounded us. They gradually herded us into a room and questioned us about what we had seen.

In the room where the police were questioning us, there was a window looking right out into the reception area, and we could still clearly see the body of David Byrne laying there. The body had not even been covered over with a sheet. It just all felt so surreal. Another victim of the shooting was taken out on a stretcher, we did not know whether the person was dead or alive. A gardai called me over to take a statement. "I would like to know what you have seen," he said. "After I have asked you a question," I replied. "Why did it take you so long to get here? The officer remained silent and repeated his original question, "what did you see? I said," I saw a gun and I just ran, that's all I have to say".

I was in shock at this point and as much as all the proof of what I had just witnessed was plain to see it all seemed like a film was playing out in front of my very eyes, only the scene would have to be cut because there was no urgency at all when the emergency services arrived, and the police never surrounded the building. It all seemed so bizarre. The entire event of what happened that day will never leave me. I looked up and just knew that Tish was looking over me that day. I could so easily of had a bullet in the back of my head. All I thought about was poor David laying there, leaving his family behind. Not an hour before we were talking and laughing about my fight a few months before. My sincere condolences go out to his family and everybody that knew him. May he rest in peace.

Once the Gardai had finished questioning everyone, people gradually started to collect their belongings from their rooms make their way to the airport. All the Box Nation production team could not wait to leave and one of the team came up to me and said we are going to arrange a flight back to London for you as soon as possible. I told them I was not going back yet, there is something I need to do so please leave my flight date booked for Monday.

I went up to my room and just lay on the bed, trying to somehow make some kind of sense of what I had just witnessed. I had left my phone in the room while I was downstairs at the weigh in so when I looked at it there were hundreds missed calls and messages. I immediately rang Candice. She answered straight away and was crying down the phone. "Are you ok, I thought something had happened to you? Little did I know but news of what had just happened went viral all around the world. She asked if I was there at the weigh in when the shooting started. I did not want to worry her, so I said no. I told her I was in my room and the show is off tomorrow but I'm not coming home yet, I am going to Connemara to visit Tish's grave. "We were so worried," she said, "but as long as you're ok".

I know what Candice was thinking. If I was boxing on that show, then she and the girls would have been there. Someone was definitely looking over me that day and I honestly believe that someone was Tish. I tried to get my head down as best I could, following the tragic and fatal experience I had just witnessed. The next morning, I put on the suit I had planned to wear for the show and made my way downstairs to the reception area, which was still cordoned off because the Gardai and forensic teams were still there gathering evidence. The hotel was in effect still a crime scene so how I was allowed to stay was a mystery to me. I managed to get out of a side door and a good friend of mine picked me up outside the Regency. "Are you ok? said my friend. "The was mad, what happened? I told him I did not want to talk about it changed the subject. We went for a bit of breakfast and then drove on to Galway. It was a rough day as we drove to Connemara. As we pulled up to Carraroe the sea was rough as the waves crashed against the rocks. I told my friend I needed 10 minutes on my own. I picked some flowers then walked over the sand and into the graveyard. The wind and the rain were so strong it nearly blew me off my feet. When I got to Tish's grave I knelt down and said to Tish, "I knew you were there yesterday looking over and protecting me". Not five minute later the rain and wind had stopped, and a beautiful rainbow formed in the sky. It was just like the one I saw when I was stuck on that rock on the Dolin beach as a small child.

I am aware how mad that sounds but whenever I'm in trouble a rainbow always seems to appear, as if someone is watching over me. As soon as I got back in the car, I got my friend to take me to Shannon Airport. I did not want to fly from Dublin because the shooting was still all over the news and the media were all over it in Dublin. I thanked my friend for taking me to see my sister and flew straight back to England. I could not wait to see Candice and the girls and give them a big cuddle. I remember thinking to myself, 'I'm staying home from now on.' All my training camps are going to be in the UK so I can come home at weekends.

Chapter 31
Meeting my long-lost family.

By now I was 38 years old and had fought all around the world including America, Canada and most of Europe. And I had spent so much time in training camps that I had missed out on so much of Marni and Shannon's life changing moments, so I decided to train closer to home from now. I found myself a gym locally and also started helping out with the kids. They reminded me of me when I first started boxing and I just wanted to give something back to the community at the same time. I was in the gym training one night when I got a phone call from a promoter I used to box for before the MGM days. The promoter, Mick Hennessy had a broadcasting deal with Channel 5 and asked if I wanted to fight on his card at the Wembley Arena on March 26. The fight was a six rounder at 11st. I was weighing around 12st 7lbs and the fight was just three weeks away, but I was confident I could make the weight so accepted the fight.

I had trained myself for the fight on the undercard of the British Middleweight title fight between Chris Eubank Jr and Nicky Blackwell. When I got to Wembley to weigh in the day before the show Mick

Hennessy came up to me and , "where's your trainer? I said I trained myself. At that moment I saw my old mate Tyson Fury with his uncle, Peter Fury. Peter's son Hughie was on the card so I said, "Don't worry Peter will work my corner". I shouted over to Peter and said 'would you be ok to work my corner tomorrow night, Peter? He just laughed and said, "yes, no problem, have you been training? Tyson turned around and said, "He only trains when he's locked into camp in the middle of nowhere like when he was with us a few years back in Holland".

Tyson looked at me and said, "do you remember that, Peter? "How can I forget," I replied. "Running 10 miles, doing press ups, burpees and sit up every half a mile, I thought I was gonna die". We were living Rocky style in the woods; how could I bloody forget that!

After weighing in I went back over to the hotel where Candice and the girls were waiting for me. Candice said, "your phone keeps ringing but no number comes up and I thought it might be important? I rang the number back and a girl answered. I said, "Hello, who is this please? "I'm your sister", came the reply. "My sister is dead". "Please don't hang up," she said, "please let me explain. When your mum left, she went on to have three other kids, you have three sisters. I want to meet you. I have come to watch you box when you were younger at York Hall". I told her, "I can't really talk now I'm fighting tomorrow night.". She said, "I know I'm coming to watch you at Wembley tomorrow. I've followed you but never had the guts to call you until now." I said, "ok, thanks for the support. I got to go now." And put the phone down.

As soon as I got off the phone Candice said, "who was that? I said, "that was my sister". I explained that my mum went on to have three more kids and I have three sisters. "What did you tell her," said Candice. "I just said that I was fighting tomorrow and had no time to talk. I feel bad now and won't sleep tonight because of this". Candice told me to ring her back and get it off your mind. I said, "Candice, the shit life I've had with my mum, I could only imagine what her life was like." Anyway, I rang her back and apologised for being so rude, it was just such a shock to know I had three sisters. We had a brief chat, and she said her name was Denise. I told her to meet me tomorrow, and we can have lunch with Candice, Shannon and Marni. "Can I bring my boyfriend? said Denise. "Of course, where do you live? I replied. "We

172

live in Essex, said Denise. "Ok, bring your overnight stuff and whatever you are wearing to the boxing and I will book you a room at the Wembley Hilton, where we are staying." Denise thanked me and we arranged to meet at 1pm the following day. I went to bed that evening and said to Candice., "I wonder what she will be like, will she like us? Then I would say something else something else until Candice said, "will you just go to sleep, you are fighting tomorrow, its three o'clock in the morning."

I woke about 8am on fight day. We had a bit of breakfast and then went on a little walk around Wembley. Then at 1pm my phone rang, and it was Denise to say they were downstairs in reception. If I am being honest, I was more nervous about meeting her than any of my previous title fights. As soon as we got out of the lift at reception, even though the reception was crowded I spotted Denise right away. She reminded me so much of Tish. We all gave each other a big cuddle and I have to say it was a very emotional time. It was the last thing I needed leading up to a fight, but you should know by now that this is just another chapter that makes up my crazy life up until now. The more I thought about having three sisters the more I needed to know about them and what they had been through.

Whilst we were having a bite to eat and getting to know each other for the first time, Tyson came into the restaurant. I shouted over, "Tyson come and meet my sister, Denise." Looking a bit puzzled, I said, "I only met her today, she's, my half-sister." Tyson looked at me and said," I can't keep with you McDonagh's, are you as wild as him? Denise just laughed. It did break the ice a bit and everyone was a bit more relaxed after that.

I told Denise I needed to get my head down and concentrate on the fight but we would meet up later to have a proper catch up. My mind was all over the place when I got Wembley but I still managed to out-point Arvydas Trizone from Lithuania over six rounds. As soon as the fight was over, I jumped in the shower and headed back over to the hotel to see Denise and her boyfriend. The main event that night was Chris Eubank Jr challenging Nicky Blackwell for his British Middleweight title. Unfortunately, Nicky collapsed in the ring afterwards and suffered a serious brain injury.

173

Once I got back to the hotel, Denise was there waiting. We bonded straight away and stayed up all night talking about our childhoods. There was plenty of tears but also plenty of laughs.

Following the victory at Wembley I pretty much ticked over for the next year as I waited for a big fight to materialise following the Dean Byrne victory. But it was now nearly two years since I won my third Irish title in Dublin and I was approaching my 40th birthday. I was offered a 10 round bout against Shayne Singleton on the undercard of the WBO heavyweight title clash between champion Joseph Parker and the then unbeaten Hughie Fury at the Manchester Arena on September 23, 2017. I accepted the fight and came out victorious over 10 hard rounds but the previous day Singleton and me got involved in an unofficial bust up at the weigh in, which resulted in the British Boxing Board of Control hitting me with an eight month ban. The ban kept me out of the ring until the middle of 2018 but that did not stop me from planning my training for a promised major title fight in the meantime.

Chapter 32

The biggest fight of my life is yet to come.

Sunday, January 29,2018 in Milton Keynes was to be my last night out before I started serious training in preparation for a major title fight. A good friend of mine, Chris Mason, was a former top level Darts player and had managed to get me some VIP tickets for the finals of one of the big televised tournaments of the year. I travelled up there with my mate Tony Discipline. We got to the hotel in the morning, which was right near the venue. So, all we had to do was walk round the corner and we were there. As soon as we got inside, I saw my old mate John McDonald, who was the Master of Ceremonies for ITV, who were broadcasting the event. After exchanging pleasantries with John, Tony and I went to the bar in the VIP area for a few pints of Guinness. All of a sudden, I seemed to lose my footing. Tony joked, "You ok Pete, you're not pissed already are you, you've only had three pints? Tony put his arm around me and laughing, repeated, "you ok?. All of a sudden, I fell sideways and went over flat on my shoulder like a dead weight. I'm not joking it happened pretty much exactly like the scene in Only Fools and Horses when Del Boy fell through the bar.

By now Tony's face had changed like the wind from sheer laughter to total panic. Every time Tony picked me up I fell down, I am sure he thought I was winding him up. Tony knows a thing or two about acting because he played the part of Tyler Moon in Eastenders a few years ago. Tony said, "Peter stops fucking about." I said, "Mate I can't stay on my feet." Tony put his arm around me and got me back to the hotel.

I laid on the bed for a bit and soon felt better. I told Tony to go back and finish watching the Darts. "No way mate," he said, "I'm staying here with you." I fell asleep. But when I woke up in the morning and got out of the bed to use the toilet, I hit every wall on the way. As soon as Tony heard all the noise he jumped out of bed and shouts," oh shit". He had stepped in a pile of sick on the floor. It was all over the place. Not just in between the beds but all over my side of the floor. As Tony was cleaning his feet, my focus was on trying to keep my balance. I was still crashing off the walls in the toilet. Once he had cleaned himself up Tony said, "right let's get you in the car and to the hospital. "I wanna go home mate," I said. "Ok, it might be your sugar level, drink some coke," said Tony. I don't know whether it was mental or physical, but it seemed like the dizziness had slowed down. I drank loads of water and managed to get home.

In the meantime, Candice had managed to get me an emergency doctors' appointment. She drove me there and the doctor conducted some tests. The doctor said she was going to send a letter to Epsom Park Hospital. "You will need to go to the Stroke Unit," said the doctor. I said OK and she handed me a letter to take with me. I put the letter in my pocket and went outside to see Candice, who was waiting in the car. She asked what the doctor had said and I just told her that because I was a professional boxer, they wanted to send me for a check up. I had not told Candice how bad I was at the Darts because she would have been worried sick. Candice said, "I have to pick the girls up now, so will drop you at the hospital and you can phone me when you're ready to be picked up."

There were so many things going through my head during that 15 minute trip to the hospital. 'Have I taken too many punches to the head in the last 30 years? Am I losing my mind? Will I remember my kids and family? Will I end up in a wheelchair?

As we pulled up at the hospital, Candice said, "why are you so quiet, you have not said a word all the way here? Candice knows me better than anyone and if you know me, I do not shut up at the best of times. I remember exactly what I had said but I made up some excuse. Once inside the hospital I found my way to the Stroke Unit and pressed the buzzer to be let in. When I got inside and walked towards the reception all I could see was old age pensioners in wheelchairs. Surely, I was too young and too healthy to be here. I handed my envelope to the lady at reception, and she said they were expecting me. A nurse came up and said, "can you please go and knock on that door over there the specialist is waiting you". I went in and sat down, and the specialist explained to me that my symptoms sounded like I had had a mini stroke

"Just to make sure, before we talk any further, I'm going to send you for an MRI scan so we can see what the problem is." she said. I was used to having and annual MRI scan when I renewed my boxing licence so I knew what to expect. It is not nice having to lay down and be sent into a tube but it is worth it in the end when you have been given the all clear. After the MRI the nurse said that they had to do another one to insert a cannular and run some dye through. For those that do not know, a cannular is a thin tube that doctors insert into a body cavity or vein to drain fluid, administer medication, or provide oxygen. I was only used to having an MRI so I asked the nurse why they needed to run a dye through my veins. She said the specialist had ask for this process so they could have a clearer picture of what is going on. Now I am thinking, 'have they seen something? Once I had a second MRI scan, I went back up to the stroke unit to speak to the specialist. He sat me down and said the good news is you have not had a stroke, but the bad news is you have a tumour on your brain. My heart just sank. The specialist said, "I can't really tell exactly what it is one hundred per cent but with the blood flowing through, it looks like it is Benign."

After hearing the word 'tumour' you can imagine, I was pretty shocked. I was just looking out of the window and staring into the sky. The specialist then informed me that they were keeping me over night and would send the results and scans to the St Georges and Atkinson Morley regional Neurological Centre. A nurse then came in, put a band on me and told me to get in a wheelchair. "I'm not getting in that," I said. "It's for insurance purposes," the nurse reasoned. "I said, "I don't care, I'm walking to the ward, no chance I'm getting used to being pushed around in that (wheelchair)."

177

Once I arrived at the ward, I looked around and there were quite a few old people just sitting around as if they were just waiting for their time to end. Being in that ward just seemed so surreal because apart from that one episode at the Darts tournament I felt very healthy. I remember sitting up in bed and thinking, 'I've got a brain tumour, this is serious, I could die'. I picked up my phone and rang Les ironman and told him I had some bad news, and that I had a brain tumour. Les had supported me from my amateur days at the Fisher and was still supporting me as a professional. Les said, "Don't worry Peter they can do amazing things now". I said, "Les, all I ask is if I die can you please make sure Candice and the kids are, ok?

"That goes without saying," said Les. Les had supported me through the good and the bad times so I knew if the unthinkable was to happen my family were to be looked out for. As soon as I got off the phone to Les, I rang Candice. She said, "Do you want me to come and pick you up? I told her they were keeping me in for tests and to get the girls looked after and to come to the Hospital. I got my good friend 'Little John' to pick Candice up and bring her to the Hospital. I wanted someone there to support her when I talked about the brain tumour, and I certainly did not want her driving.

As soon as they arrived at the ward on the third floor 'Little John' cracked a joke to break and lighten the mood. I had only been at the same ward with John a month earlier visiting his dad. Candice sat down and said, "Peter, what's the matter? There was no beating around the bush I just came out with it, "Candice, I have a brain tumour". She tried to stay strong but she just held my hand and burst into tears. It is fair to say that up until this point, life had dealt me a particularly shitty deal. And on top of everything that has happened to me so far, I am now sitting in a hospital bed with a brain tumour. But let us not forget Candice has had her fair share of heartache to deal with, too. She had survived two cancer scares, supported me without question during all my dark times, and now she's having to face up to dealing with me having a brain tumour. As soon as 'Little John' heard the bad news he just put his head in his hands in disbelief. Candice regained some composure, cuddled me and said, "you will be fine you're a fighter". I did say, though that the doctor said it looks like the tumour is Benign, which means it is not spreading and its not cancer, and is very treatable.

Candice asked if the doctor had given me any medication. I said, "no, tomorrow I'm being transferred to St Georges Hospital".

The nurse came back to check on me and said, "you will not be going to St Georges tonight so you will be staying here". I said, "Do I need any medication? The nurse replied, "no, I just need to keep you in for observation". "I'm going to discharge myself, then", I said. "I would rather give up this bed for someone that really needs. I will make my own way to St Georges tomorrow".

The nurse paused for a moment, then reluctantly agreed as long as I 'stayed home and went straight to bed'. I was hardly in any fit state to do anything else, really, was I! Lying in bed that night my brain was completely frazzled. My mind was all over the place. I just thought that my family had suffered more than our fair share of tragedy already in our lives and now this. I was worried about how Candice and the girls would cope if something happened to me. I would be lying if I said I was not feeling sorry myself. Afterall, I had been fighting all my life, one way or another, but I knew this was just another mental or physical battle that had to be won.

I woke up the next morning bright and early and made my way, with Candice, to St Georges Hospital. We arrived at the Clinic and was met by a lady with a big beaming smile across her face. "Hi Peter, I'm Vicky Barnes, I have been expecting you. I'm going to look after you, any questions you have or problems, I'm here to help you. I will help through every stage of your treatment" After hearing what Vicky had to say and seeing her smiling away, made me feel so much better and more relaxed.

Whilst I went in for some tests, Vicky stayed outside with Candice and explained to her exactly what was going to happen regarding my operation. She explained to Candice that while the procedure was far from routine, the very best surgeons were on hand and that everything will be fine. Once the tests were completed Vicky walked us across to the Atkinson Morley Wing, where the Regional Neurosciences Centre is based. The building is state of the art and one of the best equipped in the UK in dealing with neurology, neurosurgery and neurorehabilitation. I also met the surgeon, Parag Patel, who was going to perform the operation. "We have seen the scans," said Dr Patel. "The brain tumour you have is called acoustic neuroma, it's a tumour that balances on the hearing and facial nerves. The size is around three and half centimetres wide, so it's not a small one.

"We **cannot** treat with radiotherapy, the tumour is sitting on the stem of the brain. It's too dangerous as it will expand with radiotherapy treatment so we will need to operate. You will have two surgeons, myself, who will drill a hole through your skull and get you ready, and the other surgeon, who will cut the hearing nerve and balance. Unfortunately, you will lose your ability to hear in the left ear and it will never return. We will leave about five to eight millimetres of the tumour on the facial nerve. We cannot take it all because if we did, we would risk cutting the facial nerve and if that happens, the left side of your face will end up dropping".

I told the doctor that I fully understood what he had said because I had watched the operation on Youtube about twenty times. I explained that I knew what to expect and fully expected to lose my hearing in one ear and possibly my balance. Looking back on it now I must have sounded like a right know all, but I just wanted this tumour out of my head as soon as possible. Dr Patel explained that they planned to operate in about three months time. He said he was going to set up a meeting with the team performing the operation and look at how they were going to approach the procedure. Dr Patel knew I was a professional boxer. He was also an elite sportsman in his own right, having won four Commonwealth Games Gold medals representing England at Rifle Shooting. I did say that if the operation did not go to plan, he could just shoot me! Dr Patel just laughed and said," you seem confident and ready for this operation." I told him, "Doc, I had never shied away from a fight in my life, inside or outside the ring. I know this is going to be the biggest fight of my life. If you can get me in next week, I will be ready." Truth of the matter was, I was shitting myself before I got to the hospital, but Vicky and Dr Patel had put me at ease right away so I had complete confidence that the operation would be a success.

180

On March 8, I got a phone call from my consultant, Vicky to say, "Hi Pete, can you come in on March 11 for some tests to make sure you are healthy enough to go through with the operation and if all is good you will be admitted on the 13th and the operation will take place on Thursday, the 14th". I told Vicky that was all fine and myself and Candice will see her on the 11th. So, Candice called her parents Marion and John, and asked them to come over from their home on the Isle of Wight to look after Marni and Shannon. The girls knew I was going into hospital for an operation but they did not know how serious it was as we did not want to worry them. I just said it was for a routine ear operation but they are not stupid, I think they knew more than they were letting on. And if the media get wind of it would be all over the internet, anyway so they would find out for sure. Just as we were about to walk out of the door with my bags packed at around 6pm the girls came running up crying their eyes out, saying, 'Please don't go dad, we want to come.' I just cuddled them both. It was so difficult because in my head I was thinking, 'this could be the last time I see them'. I was really feeling down on the way to the hospital and never said much. My mind was just getting overloaded with the different scenarios of what could happen. You can't keep me from talking at the best of times so Candice knew there was something wrong. She kept saying to me, "are you ok? and I just kept repeating, "Yes I'm fine, I'm just getting my mind ready".

This operation was like preparing for a fight to me. I was thinking to myself, 'I'm not scared to die but I don't want to live if I don't know who anyone is. I looked at Candice and said, "I love you, please, If the operation goes wrong and I die, tell the girls every day how much I always loved them. I'm not scared of dying, only thing that scares me is coming around in the operation and not knowing who my family is and not being able to look after myself. That's not fair on you or me. Promise you would take me to Switzerland and get me the injection to end it all?

We had been through a lot of heartache and tragedy together, but this was a different level. Candice cuddled me, and said, "you are strong, you will be ok". I could see the tears running down her cheeks, and feel the emotion in her voice. It was heart breaking. I had been knocked down plenty of times in my life, not in the ring but in life, generally. This

181

was going to be the toughest 12 rounds of my life. I only know one way to fight and that is to get straight back up and keep fighting.

On the way to the hospital, we picked up my pal 'Little John'. If things were going to go wrong, I did not want Candice coming home on her own. In any case 'Little John' is a funny fella and he soon had us laughing as soon as he got in the car. He soon took our minds off things. I said, "John, I got my leprechaun outfit with me. Do you wanna put it on to bring me good luck? Once we got to the hospital we were met by Tony, my mate that was with me when I collapsed at the Darts. I wanted my operation to be filmed so I asked Tony to film it. He brought an entire bloody camera crew with him! I just wanted to help people to understand and experience what it was like to go through a brain tumour operation. I know it sounds crazy, but thousands of people and families go through what I was through every day, and if just one person could see how it all worked and get a greater understanding of how the procedure worked then it would be worth it.

My first boxing trainer George Woodman and his identical twin brother Andrew, turned up at the hospital as well. They knew me when I first come to England as a snotty nosed six-year-old. They were devastated when they found out about my illness and came straight to the hospital. We had a long chat about the good old days training at the Fisher. We were having such a good laugh I completely forgot to go to the second floor of the Atkinson Morley Wing. I said my goodbyes to George and Andrew, and they asked what time was the operation? I told them it was at 9am and they promised to be there waiting when I come back to the ward. In the meantime Tony was making inquiries about filming the operation. We made our way up to my private room and Tony came in and said, "We have to ask in the morning if it is ok to film the entire operation but it was ok to film in my rooms I'm going to start filming now. And I will be up in the morning to film you before you go down to theatre." A few hours later Candice and 'Little John' went home. I was on the steroids from the Monday to help reduce the swelling of the tumour and I was eating like a horse. I was so full of energy I could not sleep. Every hour on the hour the nurse would come in and monitor my health. I think the adrenaline together with so much going through my mind was keeping me awake. I also have a very active mind, always thinking about things so I do not suppose that helped much. Maybe that's why I talk so much! Every five minutes I was either looking at the clock or looking out of the window watching the sun come up. In between that I was also filming video messages for the kids as well. No one has seen those videos to this day. I thought if I die or lost my memory, then the girls have those memories to watch whenever they chose to.

My mind was so preoccupied throughout the night that 7am soon came around and Vicky Barnes came flying in through the door. Quick as a flash Vicky said, 'are you ready Pete?' It reminded me of when I was boxing in a televised boxing show and the TV producer comes in and says, 'live in five, are you ready?'

Vicky said, "It's going to be busy for the next hour, how did you sleep?' I said I had not slept all night. Vicky was always positive and had this big comforting smile on her face. I always felt at ease when she explained things to me. "don't worry you can sleep when your down there on the table." That reassuring big smile appeared again moments later when she said, "Why are you dressed like a Leprechaun? Pete, you're crazy". I explained that when I used to fight, I sometimes wore a Leprechaun outfit. And that as it was St Patricks day, and my sister's birthday on Sunday I would wear my outfit. I also told Vicky I will be going home on Sunday as well to celebrate Tish's birthday with a nice cold pint of Guinness. Vicky laughed and said, "We will see. Maybe not on Sunday" "I promise I will be," I replied. At that moment, Candice came in the room accompanied by Tony and his cameraman. No sooner had the camera started rolling, in walks a smartly dressed man in a suit. I presume he was the hospital solicitor because he then started reading a disclaimer type letter to me. Something along the lines of 'If this operation goes wrong, if you die, if you end up brain damaged, etc'. The letter was far more professional and official than that, but you get the idea. Anyway, the 'solicitor' got some way through the letter when I interrupted. "Stop right there. If I end up brain damaged, I'm off to Switzerland for the injection". The gentleman in the suit replied, "that is something you will have to speak to a lawyer about". I looked at Candice and said, "remember the deal we had".

After a short discussion I signed the paperwork and said, "Let's get this done". With that, in came two anaesthetists. They explained what the

183

plan was for the operation and their job role. To add to the Leprechaun theme, everyone that entered the room received a gold coin. Imagine their disappointment when they realised it was chocolate! The next two people to enter my now crowded room was Dr Patel and Dr Martin, the two men, whom I entrusted my future wellbeing with. As soon as Dr Martin saw the cameraman filming away, he immediately shouted, "you can turn that off, I don't want any filming when I'm in the room". I guess that answered my question then. If the doc did not want any filming in the room there was no chance of filming in the operating theatre.

Both doctors explained that the operation will take between six and eight hours to perform as long as there were no complications. I think that's when it sunk in for me that this was no routine operation. Dr Martin said "You will then be moved to intensive care to recover and for observation. Then, if all is well you will be moved back to this room for a further twenty four hours". Looking me up and down, Dr Martin continued, "will you be wearing the Leprechaun suit into the operating theatre? "Of course," I replied. After saying my goodbyes to Tony and 'Little John', Candice and her mum walked with me to the operating theatre. It was quite surreal walking along the corridors. I was like one of my ring walks, a bit like walking into battle. Once we got to the theatre door, I said goodbye to Candice, who tried really hard to hold back the tears. Going through those doors, taking off my outfit and climbing onto the operating table felt just like climbing through the ropes, only you could hear a pin drop in that place.

As the anaesthetists prepared to sedate me, one said, "we will count to 10 but you will probably be asleep by five". I laughed and said, "I don't think so. I have never been knocked down or out in sparring or a fight so good luck with that! It took three attempts to put me asleep ,before I was eventually out cold. I bet they were glad; it was the only way to stop me talking!

It goes without saying that the brain is a very complex part of the human body. Now, I'm no expert, far from It, but it seems to me that the brain is the engine room that sends messages and signals to the rest of your body, and that's how we function day to day. And of course, we are all unique in our own way. Once I was put to sleep, this is how my brain seemed to work while I was being operated on.

What I remember is this. I was trying to come round and could hear faint voices in the background. I was unzipping my body bag and then found myself removing myself from another one, and so on. I was getting colder and colder as I kept removing myself from these bags. It was really dark. I was shouting, 'Ref'. I'm getting up and looking for my gumshield. Then the light started to shine through like I was looking up at the lights above the boxing ring. Then I heard, 'get up, get up'. I said, 'I will in a minute'. I shouted, 'George where's my gumshield? I knew George and Andrew were there I could hear their voices from the corner. Then George said, 'your Nurse is a good looker, Pete'. They both started laughing. I then started to wake up and everything went blank. The next thing I know, I woke up in intensive care with cables and tubes coming out of every orifice.

I am still not sure if it was just blind panic or because I felt restricted, but I just started pulling at all the wires and tubes. Nurses quickly rushed over to calm me down but all I kept saying was, 'I want to go home'. I was making such a fuss the nurse had to restrain me and knock me out again with a sedative. I think I was out for about three hours. Once I woke up again, Candice and her dad, John were sitting by my bedside just staring at me. As grumpy as you like I said, "what you two looking at? John laughed and replied, "oh no Pete's back". "What am I doing here? I replied.

Candice explained, "there were some complications with the operation. You were in there for 15 hours, the tumour kept bleeding. But its ok because the operation was very successful." Apparently, the average time for this type of operation is between eight and 12 hours, just my luck to be in there for 15. Once the nurses were satisfied, I was making progress, I was moved back my private room.

I was in that much pain I could not even lift my head off the pillow. I said to Candice, George and Andrew were there when I came out of the operation? She said, "yes, they were". What a relief that was because now I know my brain was working ok. "I remember everything they said," I told Candice. "I said I was wearing a gumshield". She confirmed that is what they told her. I was so happy that my mind was ok so now I can concentrate on my recovery.

185

"Vicky is coming to see you tomorrow to get you out of bed," said Candice. "I'm not waiting for Vicky," I said. "I'm ready to go now. Come on, grab that Catheter bag, let's go for a walk? Candice was totally against me venturing out unaided so quickly after such a big operation but me being the stubborn and determined so and so that I am, insisted. "Grab that bag, Candice. If you don't, I will drag it with me". It took me about five minutes to get out of bed and put my feet on the floor. I took about two steps and immediately did an impression of Bambi, trying to walk for the first time. I was all over the place. Candice insisted I get back to bed and rest. "But I want to go home," I said. As always, Candice was right when she replied, "you need to rest and this is the best place for you at the moment, so get some sleep. You will need all your energy for when Vicky comes back tomorrow".

Tomorrow could not come fast enough for me. The next day at 8am on March 15, a Friday, Vicky popped in as arranged to see how I was progressing. With that beaming smile Vicky said, "How you are doing Pete". "I just want to go home," I said in an abrupt like tone. "Well, that's a little while yet," she said. "But why? I reasoned. "The first thing we need to do is take the Catheter out so you will feel some pain", Vicky said. She was not bloody lying. I'm not joking, Vicky gently pulled out the Catheter and I screamed like I had just been burnt with a hot poker. I had never felt pain like it in my life. Vicky insisted I sat down and relaxed for a while, and for once I did exactly as I was told. Those you that have had the misfortune of experiencing a major operation will be aware that there is a check list to go through before you can go home. Shortly after experiencing the most physically painful moment of my life my surgeons Dr Patel and Dr Martin came in to see me and check me over. "How are you feeling Peter? Said Dr Martin. After checking my stitches, which ran from the front of my left ear all the way round the back of my head, Dr Martin said, "your operation took a lot longer than most, about 15 hours. Your tumour bled quite a bit so it was tricky to cut out but it was very successful in the end and you're looking well". I told Dr Martin what I told Vicky, "I want to be home by St Patricks Day". Dr Patel said, "That may not be possible because we have a lot to test you on. We will see you again on Monday".

Once they had gone Vicky came in and I insisted that I wanted to start these tests now. "The sooner we start these tests the sooner you can get rid of me," I said with a cheeky smile. "Ok," said Vicky, "can you get out of bed? I did not need telling twice, I thought, 'right let's go'. As soon as I put my feet on the floor, I did wobble a bit, less like Bambi this time but more like the Grandad from Charlie and the Chocolate Factory, so it was a slight improvement.

Vicky held my arm for support and said, "I will assist you and see how we get on". It took a bit of time but, eventually we got outside the room and into the corridor. I started but it was a bit weird because I had lost my hearing in the left ear, so my balance was all over the place. I could hear noises but did not know what direction they were coming from. As I walked up and down past intensive care assisted by Vicky, I said, Vicky let me go? She said, "No Pete it's too soon". In my best begging voice, I said, "please? Reluctantly, Vicky let me go, but she was still right there waiting to catch me if I fell. At that moment Dr Patel came walking past and saw me walking unassisted. "That's amazing", he said. "To come out of a major 15-hour operation and walking on your own a day later, you may prove us all wrong".

"I did tell you so," I said, with a cheeky grin on face. "I'm going home now to have a drop of Guinness to celebrate my sister's birthday". My test was not over yet. There was no way Vicky was letting me off that lightly. "Now the stairs," she said. "Go up and down a flight of stairs, but make sure you hold on to the bannisters at all times".

I started walking up the stairs and Vicky was right behind me. Once I got to the top, Vicky said, "now back down again". "Now we do it my way," I said. So, I walked down the stairs without holding on to anything. Poor Vicky looked more nervous than me but when I got down to the bottom, safely, she said, "You are so going home on Sunday".

I was so pleased but when I went back to the room and got on to the bed my head was pounding. Vicky got me some powerful painkillers and I slept like a baby. That must have been a relief to everyone, not having me going on no stop in their ears!

I woke up on the 16th and did a more exercise but there was still one more hurdle to jump, and that was to go to the toilet. Of course, to go the toilet is a normal bodily function that we all take for granted but I had a Catheter fitted and taken out and was having a problem going. I was given so many different medications to make me go that when I eventually did, I nearly passed out. I thought removing the Catheter was painful but, wow, that was nothing compared to weeing naturally for the first time in ages. It was that painful even all these years later I can still tell you exactly what and day it was. The exact time was 8.25pm on Saturday, March 16. I now understand why women always remember the exact time their baby is born. I can fully respect what a woman has to go through when in labour, and will leave it there.

I was still getting the incredibly painful headaches and I could not sleep, waiting for the sun to come up. The doctor came in and signed me out at 9am. Candice and my girls, Shannon and Marni were already there waiting for me. I was already dressed, proudly wearing my Leprechaun outfit. It was St Patricks Day and I had achieved my objective of going home on Tish's birthday. I was so happy but sad at the same time. We made our way out through the hospital corridors, signed all the paperwork and pick up all the medication I needed. It was a funny feeling walking out of the hospital and into the fresh air. Sounds crazy but it felt similar to when I breathed the fresh air of a free man when I walked out of the Old Bailey after being acquitted of attempted murder all those years ago.

As I had lost the hearing in my left ear everything felt different, the car noises, planes overhead, people talking in the background. When I first got in the car it felt like a roller coaster, fast and bumpy. My head was spinning when I got home. Candice's mum and dad had decorated the place with 'Welcome home champ' banners and the girls had made cakes. Candice poured me an ice cold can of Guinness to drink a toast to Tish. It was lovely to be home but taking a mouthful of that that Guinness made me feel sick. Just laying on my couch and sleeping in my own bed felt great. We had a lot of visitors over the next four days, and I really appreciated people coming to see me but I it just made me so tired.

On March 21 I told Candice that I would like to go with her to pick Marni up from school. She said she would ring the school to see if we could park inside so I could lean on the car. "No," I said, "I want to surprise her by walking up to her class. With the help of Candice holding my arm I walked up to her class, and it was so worth it to see her smiling face come running up to me and giving me a big cuddle. A few of the mums came up to me and asked how I was, and what my plans were being as I could not fight any more. I told them, "I've had a crazy life so maybe a book (this one) or a film can be made. There's not much more that can happen now except death". Hopefully, those ladies at the school gates will read this now and know I kept my word.

Chapter 33
More family tragedy

Seeing Marni so happy as we walked out of the school gates and back to the car was worth all the effort and time it took for me to walk just a few yards across the school playground. We got back in the car, and no sooner had I put my seatbelt on and asked Marni about her day, than Candice's phone rang. It was Liam's girlfriend and she sounded distressed and all over the place. Candice said," What's up". All Liam's girlfriend kept saying was, "He's dead, he's dead". Candice, "no he's not, he's here next to me". "Not Pete, Liam, his older brother". Then she put the phone down. Not 10 minutes earlier I had that conversation with some of the mums at the school about 'not much more can happen in my crazy life', and now we get a call to say Liam's dead.

We drove straight home and never mentioned a word until we knew more. In any case, we certainly did not want to upset Marni, she did not know what had happened and we did not want to upset her. I was still coming to terms with my own recent illness and operation, so you can imagine how shocked I was to hear the latest devastating news. We got home and my younger brother Martin rang. He said, "Have you heard the news?
"About Liam? I spoke. "
Yes, he took his own life," said Martin.

"When?

"They are saying this morning," explained Martin. "He rang work and said he would be in very soon but when he did not turn up after about an hour one of the staff got worried and went to his house. His work van was still outside so he rang the police, and they turned up and broke in. They found him hanging by a rope from the stairs."

I had not seen Liam for a while and did not have his address so I got Martin to find out where he lived. Once it was all confirmed that Liam had taken his own life I phoned his wife, Jean and the rest of the family. The one person I could not tell was my dad. I just could not bring myself to tell him. He had already put a daughter in the ground, and he was probably still getting his head around my potentially life-threatening operation, so the last thing he needed was to hear Liam had taken his own life. I was also worried about how Liam had killed himself because Dad knew Liam had witnessed him trying to do the same thing many years before.

Although they were separated, Liam's wife Jean was his next of kin, so I had to speak to her and make sure the police did not go to my dad's house and tell him the cause of death. I then rang a good friend of mine, 'Frank the Shank', and asked him if he could do me favour and drive me over to Maidstone in Kent, where Liam was staying. I explained the situation and Frank said, "I did not know he was not well, sorry to hear that". I said, "If he was not well, I never knew". The one thing I did know, though, was, Liam never got over the death of our sister, Tish. They were only a year apart in age and were more like twins. They drifted apart a bit as they got older, like a lot of families. They were so close as kids and a bit older than me and Martin, so they saw a lot more of how toxic our mum was than we did.

While I was on my way to Maidstone, I spoke to Frank about all the fun times I had with Liam. How he first introduced me to the Fisher Boxing Club, and how we used to put socks on our hands and box in the living room at home. He's the one that toughened me up. He would make me cry but I just kept coming at him and never gave up. As we got older, and I was taking boxing more serious he did not want to play anymore. I don't blame him. I told Frank that without Liam I probably would never have put on a pair of boxing gloves.

After driving halfway around the M25 we eventually reached Liam's house, which was by now all boarded up. I got out of the car and just gazed up at the window on the first floor. I suppose I was staring as much into space as I was looking up at the window. Maybe I was experiencing the shock of it all. I remember thinking to myself, 'Why Liam, could you not have come and spoken to me? Liam had cut himself off from me when he left his wife Jean and his kids, two years previously. But he did ring Candice just before I went into hospital. I always ask myself, 'if I had died, would Liam still be here? To this day I do not know why I went to his house, maybe it made me feel closer to him. Prior to getting the phone call to say he had killed himself I did not even know where he lived.

The next day I went to visit my dad to inform him of Liam's passing. He still lives in Bermondsey and loves it there. A proper Irish Londoner is my dad. It was really hard to lie to my dad about how Liam really died because he had used the same method many years before in a bid to take his own life, not once but twice. Instead, I told dad that Liam had died from a reaction to some tablets he was taking. I'm pretty sure he did not believe me because even now, a few years later he still asks, 'how did Liam die?

I can only imagine what goes through my dad's mind. He is 83 years old. He brought up four kids on his own and even after everything my mum put him and us kids through, he still loves her. He speaks about how broken hearted he is, losing two children. Nobody said life was fair, but I just wish us McDonagh's could get a little bit of a break sometimes. A little over four weeks after Liam took his own life and nearly five since I came through a potentially life changing operation, the day came to put Liam to rest. It was April 11, 2019 and the doctors had told me in no uncertain terms, that I was not to be help carry Liam's coffin. I told the doctors that if I die carrying Liam then so be it. I was determined to carry my brother into Church, and to his final resting place, even if I needed help to balance. It was yet another emotional day for our family. Shannon wrote a lovely poem for Liam and read it out in the Church. She was so brave to do that, and I was very proud of her. My girls had already lost their aunt Tish and now an uncle passed away as well. Liam loved those girls. In fact, Shannon was the image of

192

both Tish and Liam, the resemblance was that similar. In fact, some people thought Liam was her father.

Liam was cremated, and I always promised that when I was healthy again, I would take Liam's ashes and bury them with Tish. That promise was fulfilled on December 15, 2022. A few weeks after the operation I was starting to feel quite a bit better, but I just could not get my head around why Liam had taken his own life. I kept ringing people, trying to find out why he did what he did, but it was not until we attended the inquest that many of the questions were answered. The statement read out made for shocking reading. Liam's girlfriend said that from time to time, he would come downstairs with a plastic bag over his head with gaffer tape round his neck in an attempt to suffocate himself. She also revealed that the scaffold board and rope he eventually used to hang himself with, was in the loft and ready to use at least two months before he died. I would like to think that I could have helped him, and I am sad we never stayed in touch, but you know what? He chose to take his life and I honestly think that if someone is that determined then they will succeed. I hope he is happy and at peace now, there with my sister. Pretty much every day is a struggle for me, mentally, but thinking about those two together is what keeps me fighting on.

As 2020 approached my recovery was improving much slower than I would have liked. I just felt like I was taking one step forward and two steps backwards. In the space of less than two years I had gone from traveling the world, taking part in training camps, to the everyday struggle of physiotherapy sessions and hardly ever leaving the house. Then, in March 2020 I was struck down with Covid 19. I was confined to my bed for two weeks. At one point I honestly thought I was going to die. Believe me, if anyone thinks Covid 19 is not real, I can assure you it really is. I was that worried about dying that I emailed my solicitor to make out a Will and leave everything I owned to my girls. Luckily, I managed to recover. Around this time, I was still having regular MRI scans every three months. Then in early 2021, an MRI scan showed that the tumour had started growing again and growing fast. I had a consultation with my surgeon, Dr Patel, and he explained to me that only five percent of these tumours ever grow back. Now, I know life has dealt me a few shitty cards in this life, but surely, I was due a change in fortune now? Not on your life, I should have known I'd be in that five percent!

After looking at all the X rays and reading all the notes, Dr Patel decided I was to have radiotherapy treatment. "We do not do radiotherapy here," said Dr Patel, "so I'm going to refer you to the Royal Marsden. You will undergo cyber knife treatment. The machine will pinpoint where the tumour is and work on it. It's an amazing machine with great results".

A week or so later I got a call from the Royal Marsden to say I had been booked in for a scan. The last time I was at the Royal Marsden was about three years ago when I did some charity work, we raised some money to buy presents for one the children in the cancer ward. I never in my wildest dreams thought that I would be coming back here and going through treatment, myself.

The person in charge of the MRI unit explained that I was going to have to have a mask fitted before I could have the scan. So, they escorted me to this room, where there was a what I can only describe as a state-of-the-art robot. I said to the consultant, "what's that? She replied, "That's the machine that will doing your radiotherapy. It's what is called a Cyber Knife". I was then asked to lay down on this table, where they place this plastic mesh type mask on your face. The mask sort of warms up and moulds to your skin. It was a bit like putting your finger in hot wax that moulds round your finger. It then gets stretched and clamped down onto the table, which shapes the mask exactly to your face. The machine then draws marks for your eyes and mouth, and then points to where the target of the radiotherapy will go. It is a really clever machine.

A week or so after the fitting for my mask I went back to the Royal Marsden for my radiotherapy treatment. Although I had already experienced my face being clamped to the table for the mask fitting it still felt strange because this time I had to remain totally still while the Cyber Knife Robot did its job, pinpointing the exact area to be treated. I did feel quite a bit of dizziness and suffered a thumping headache afterwards, but these were all natural side effects from the treatment. Well, it is not everyday your brain gets zapped with massive shots of radiation. I was allowed to keep the mask as a souvenir. Some people like to paint them so I thought, as Marni loves her art and is pretty creative, I took it home for her to work her magic on. The road to recovery now starts all over again.

Chapter 34
Recovery and life without boxing.

Ever since I was diagnosed with a brain tumour in March 2019, I have struggled to come to terms with the loss of hearing in my left ear and my balance not being as good as it used to be. I would be lying if I said my confidence has not been affected. I was going to get back into boxing punditry on TV, and was also looking at working with Les again at the Fish Market, but because of my hearing loss and lack my balance not being what it used be, not so sure working with sharp knives and wet floors would be a such a good idea. I'm not so good with background noise nowadays, either so not show how that would work commentating at ringside. I was invited to Pakistan in January, 2022 to be involved in a professional boxing event. That trip was a serious eye opener. Although we were escorted everywhere by security forces, the event was a great success, and we were made very welcome. Maybe I will go back in 2023 to promote this book!

I was also honoured by the Word Boxing Council for my achievements as a professional boxer. I was presented with the famous green belt at a charity dinner last September at the Silver mere Golf course in Surrey by my good friend and former world boxing champion Ricky Hatton. With Ricky's help we managed to raise a quite a bit of money for Niamh's Next Step, a children's Cancer charity and for former boxer Charlie Wynn, who is now wheelchair bound due to an injury he sustained in the boxing ring.

I am also very proud of my daughter's Shannan and Marni. Shannan has finished her GCSE's and will be going into the 6th form. She has worked so hard and gained top marks in all her exams as well as studying at drama at the Italia Conti School of performing Arts. Marni is 12 years old and now in year 8 at Secondary School. She is doing really well and is a Cheerleader, where she performs all over the country.

After witnessing how impressive and how well looked after I was during my operation , Candice decided to have a career change and now works for the NHS.

I also promised myself that after Liam passed away, as soon as I was well enough, I would take his Ashes back to Connemara and lay him to rest with our sister, Tish. I am pleased to say I was able to fulfil that promise on December 09, 2022. We opened a small part of the grave with a shovel and placed the ashes there so they can now rest in peace together.

Chapter 35

My final thoughts.

As I arrived at her graveside, all my memories of them came flooding back and the tears ran down my cheeks faster than an Olympic skier in a downhill slalom race. As I dug the hole and peered into it, I knew it was time for me to seek out professional help so I could move on with my life. I have not got boxing anymore to numb the pain but just putting pen to paper to tell my story has allowed me to go some way to exercise my demons.

If nothing else, I hope Irish Blood and Grit will inspire and help vulnerable people understand that if you get knocked down you can always get back up again and not be afraid to ask for help.

I have already started writing the sequel to this book and I am really going to open up and explain in more detail of how I am recovering. Unfortunately, I have some more bad news. During one of my many routine scans in March, 2023 at the Royal Marsden Hospital, I was informed that my tumour has started growing again. I have been fighting one way or another all my life so one more battle is not going to bother me. That's the top and bottom of it, really. I hope this book helps and inspires others going through very difficult times and makes them realise that hard times do not always last forever unless of course, your name happens to be Peter McDonagh.

As I write these last few lines to close this particular chapter in my life it is fair to say that life has not dealt the McDonagh's of Connemara the greatest of hands, you only have to skip through one chapter of this book to work that out. My dad, Bill is still going strong and living in Bermondsey and I try and keep track of my little brother, Martin as best I can. He is doing great looking after my dad and my two nephews Josh and Billy. I have to admit I still struggle with my mental health on a daily basis because of it. And because of the 15-hour operation to remove my tumour I will also struggle physically for the rest of my life. But you know what? I am still here fighting, and I cannot thank Dr's Martin and Patel enough for performing such a successful operation, and of course the amazing Vicky Barnes, for looking after me so well. Because of them I am still here and I get to spend time quality time with my lovely wife, Candice and my beautiful daughters. Candice is my rock, my best friend, and she really does deserves a medal for putting up with me. Shannon and Marni were my biggest fans when I was boxing but I am their biggest cheerleader now, and am so proud of them. I will keep fighting and making the best life I can.

Printed in Great Britain
by Amazon